THE PRACTICAL GUIDE TO MODERN MUSIC THEORY FOR GUITARISTS

Third Edition

JOSEPH ALEXANDER

FUNDAMENTAL CHANGES

The Practical Guide to Modern Music Theory for Guitarists

Third Edition

Published by **www.fundamental-changes.com**

ISBN:978-1-911267-77-5

www.fundamental-changes.com

Twitter: **@guitar_joseph**

Over 10,000 fans on Facebook: **FundamentalChangesInGuitar**

Instagram: **FundamentalChanges**

Contents

Introduction

The most common statement I hear as a private guitar teacher is, "I need to learn guitar theory..."

Consider what that means to you. Why will you benefit from knowing guitar theory? What will you do with it? How will it make you a better player? What is your actual *goal*?

My belief is that the statement has a couple of flaws. Firstly, what is *guitar* theory? The guitar is a musical instrument and there is no specific *guitar* theory. What I will teach you in this book is *music theory* as it applies to the guitar, from a guitarist's point of view.

A guitarists, we quite rightly approach music (and music theory), in a different way from a classical pianist. When we solo we mainly use *pentatonic* and *modal* scales, so our musical perspective does not necessarily begin from the Major and Melodic Minor scales as it might if we were classically trained. The first scale most guitar players learn on the guitar is the *Minor Pentatonic*. It's the root sound, even after we have explored more advanced concepts.

Today is the day to stop thinking of yourself as a guitarist who plays music. You are a musician who plays the guitar.

It is important to remember that music theory is simply a way to communicate ideas. Just because classical and rock players may explain an idea differently, doesn't mean that one is wrong. It just means they have a different perspective and each is useful in different ways.

My second issue with the statement, "I need to learn guitar theory" is that there is no point in knowing any theory unless you can apply it musically.

Imagine for a second that you knew all the rules of English grammar: You knew all about pronouns, the subjunctive, prepositions and modal verbs etc. Imagine you knew all that, but you never learned to speak. That's a good analogy for studying theory without learning the vocabulary to apply it. What kind of musician do you want to be?

I'm writing this book because I feel there is a tendency for guitarists to know theory, but not how to make music with it. In this book I give real, constructive examples of everything that is covered. If you only know the theory and not how to put it into practice, it's a bit like asking someone to describe the colour blue. Isn't it easier to have a little blue in your palette just to show them?

There are many ways to describe the ideas in this book. I hope the way I approach and demonstrate each subject works for you. There are audio tracks for every important concept which you can download from **www.fundamental-changes.com** for free. I highly recommend that you get these audio examples as they really help the book come to life.

It is important that you hear each concept in context, even if you don't immediately understand the idea. You'll be surprised how much you can pick up through just listening. Music is about sounds and feelings, not words on paper, so don't panic if an idea seems complex at first. If all else fails, email me via the website and I'll do my best to answer your questions.

Get the Audio

The audio files for this book are available to download for free from **www.fundamental-changes.com** and the link is in the top right corner. Simply select this book title from the drop-down menu and follow the instructions to get the audio.

We recommend that you download the files directly to your computer, not to your tablet, and extract them there before adding them to your media library. You can then put them on your tablet, iPod or burn them to CD. On the download page there is a help PDF and we also provide technical support via the contact form.

Kindle / eReaders

To get the most out of this book, remember that you can double tap any image to enlarge it. Turn off 'column viewing' and hold your kindle in landscape mode.

Thanks to **Quist** for providing all the excellent backing tracks for this book.

Part One – Major Scale Construction, Chords and Harmony

Part One of this book discusses the 'basics' of Western music. It's essential to understand these concepts before moving on to Part Two, where we discuss the *modes* of the Major scale and the layered approaches we can take when soloing with them.

In Part One, we examine how scales are constructed, what makes them unique, their harmonisation (chords), and transposing progressions into different keys. We also learn how musicians communicate with a standardised language based on Roman numerals and how to accurately name the different notes in a scale.

What is a Scale?

A scale is a series of steps between two fixed musical points. These two fixed points are always the same note, but in different *octaves*. For example, these points could both be the note 'C', one being higher in pitch than the other:

Example 1a:

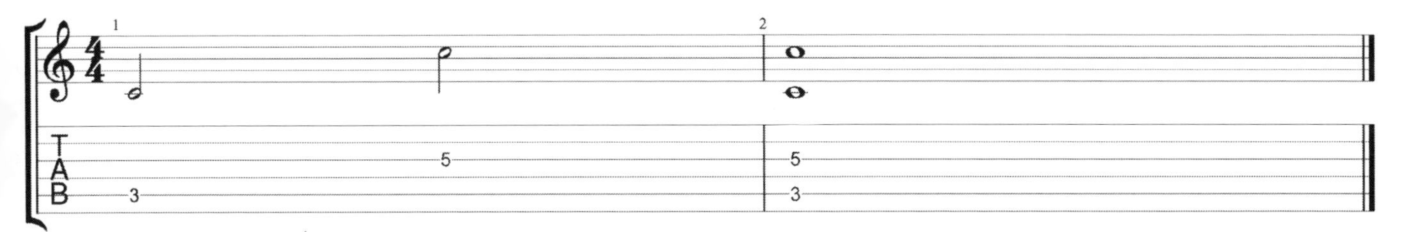

(Go to **www.fundamental-changes.com** now to get all the audio examples and backing tracks for this book).

Listen to the above example, You can hear that while the notes are fundamentally the same, they are at a different *pitch*. A scale is simply a way to break up the space in between these notes.

One way to think about this is to imagine a ladder where the first and last rungs are fixed, but you can change the spacings of any of the rungs in between. Some spaces may be smaller, some larger, but however you arrange them, you will always end up at the same fixed point once you've climbed the ladder. It is this arrangement of the notes that makes each scale sound different and gives them a different musical feeling.

The rungs on the ladder are the notes that we play, and the spaces between the rungs are the distances between these notes. These distances are measured in *tones* and *semitones* – two semitones are equal in distance to one tone.

Once you have 'set' the rungs of your ladder, you can carry your ladder to any different location (note) and set it down somewhere new. In the same way, any scale of the same *type* always has the same pattern of tones and semitones, no matter what your starting note is.

For example, the pattern of tones and semitones is the same whether you're playing the scale of C Major, F# Major, Bb Major or any other *Major* scale. Each scale of the same type always has the same pattern.

The Major Scale

Overview

Although it is not one of the most interesting scales for guitarists to use, the Major scale has been the fundamental building block of western harmony for the past 800 years. Most of the chords you hear in music are formed from this scale. It is essential to understand how this scale works because its step pattern or *formula* is the yardstick by which we describe *any* other musical sound.

The Major scale is used in rock, but often its extremely happy vibe is a bit too bright for us. However, check out **Friends** by Joe Satriani for a truly triumphant Major scale feeling.

Other tunes you shuld check out are:

- **Jessica** by the Allman Brothers
- The main theme from **Cliffs of Dover** by Eric Johnson (this kicks in at 2:32)
- **Like a Rolling Stone** by Bob Dylan

Often, melodies are written using the Major scale, before a guitar solo is played in a Minor key to create a rockier sound, for example **Jump** by Van Halen

It is important to understand how the Major scale functions, and how to create melody and harmony from it before launching into the rest of this book, so make sure you are comfortable with the ideas below before moving on to part two.

Construction

Returning to our ladder analogy: the sound or *flavour* of the Major scale is due to the way the rungs are spaced between the two fixed points at each end. In other words, there is a set pattern of tones and semitones that gives the Major scale its unique quality. Let's discover what they are.

In the scale of C Major there are no sharps or flats, and if you were playing a keyboard you would begin and end on the note C, and play only the white notes (no black ones).

The notes, therefore, in the scale of C Major are;

C D E F G A B

The note C is the *root* of the scale and often referred to as the *tonic*.

You may be used to playing scales on the guitar across the neck, however to to understand how the patterns of tones and semitones in the ladder are set, we will examine this scale played along one string:

Example 2a:

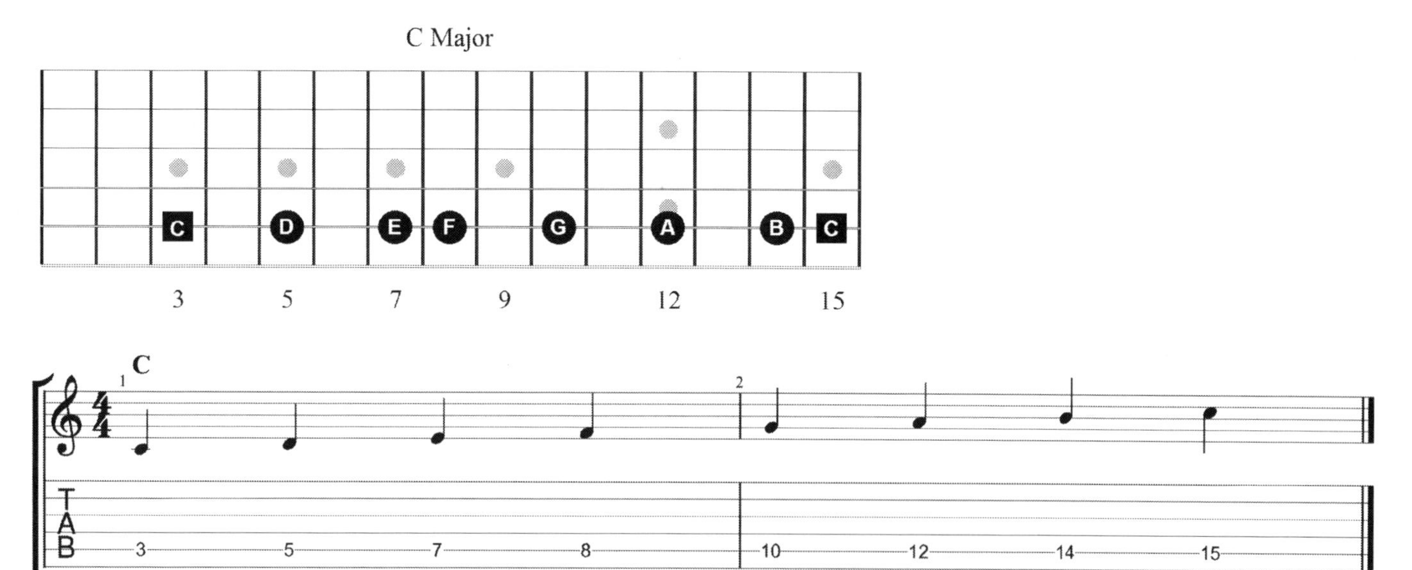

Each fret distance on the guitar is one semitone, so two frets is equal to one tone.

When the scale is laid out on a neck diagram, it is clear to see that the distance between some notes is one tone, and between others it is one semitone. The distance between the notes C and D is one tone, and between E and F it is one semitone.

Listen to, and play example 2a now. Memorise this pattern as it forms the basis of everything that follows.

The previous diagram shows the ladder for the Major scale. Wherever we place the first note, the pattern of tones and semitones must always remain the same if we are to create the exact sound of the Major scale. If we change the pattern, it is no longer a Major scale.

The set pattern is as follows:

Tone, Tone, Semitone, Tone, Tone, Tone, Semitone.

C – D Tone

D – E Tone

E – F Semitone

F – G Tone

G – A Tone

A – B Tone

B – C Semitone.

This pattern is an important building block of all music. It always forms the same pattern of T T St T T T St.

It is given the formula:

1 2 3 4 5 6 7

Simple as that may seem, we use this formula to help describe every other scale. For example, later in this book you will see the formula:

1 2 3 #4 5 6 7

This is a shorthand way of saying that this scale is identical in every way to the Major scale, except that the 4th note has been *sharpened* (#) by a semitone.

The original scale of C Major contained the notes

C D E F G A B C

So the #4 in the second formula tells us that the notes would be

C D E F# G A B C

(1 2 3 #4 5 6 7 is actually the formula for the Lydian mode, but you don't need to know that yet).

Construction of the Major Scale in Other Keys

To form the Major Scale in the key of C, we simply started on the note C and ran alphabetically through the notes until we got back to our starting point. Let's test this concept by starting on a different note, for example, G:

G A B C D E F G

We can check to see if the rungs on our ladder are the same. Remember the Major scale pattern:

Tone, Tone, Semitone, Tone, Tone, Tone, Semitone.

G – A = Tone

A – B = Tone

B – C = Semitone

C – D = Tone

D – E = Tone

E – F = **Semitone**

F – G = **Tone**

Hopefully you can already see that there is a problem with the pattern of tones and semitones over the last 2 notes, F and G.

This is easier to see on the guitar neck.

Example 3a:

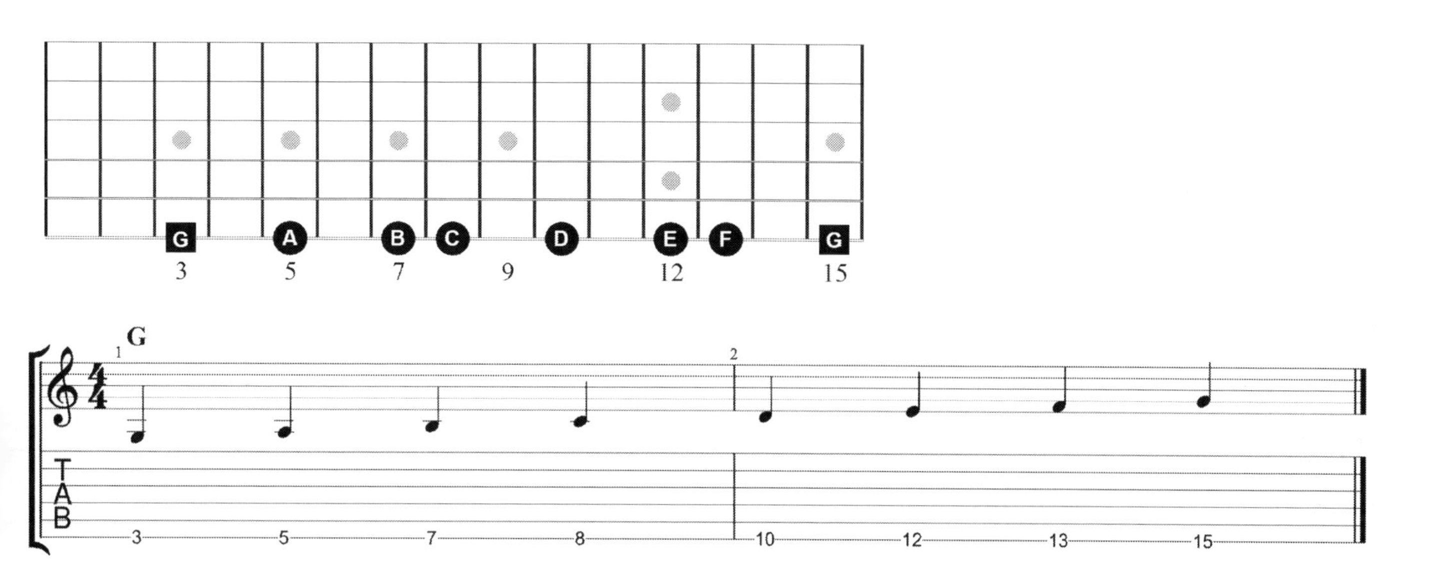

Play through this example and listen to how it sounds. Can you hear something that doesn't belong in a Major scale?

The last rung on the ladder should be a semitone, and the one before that should be a tone, like this:

Example 3b:

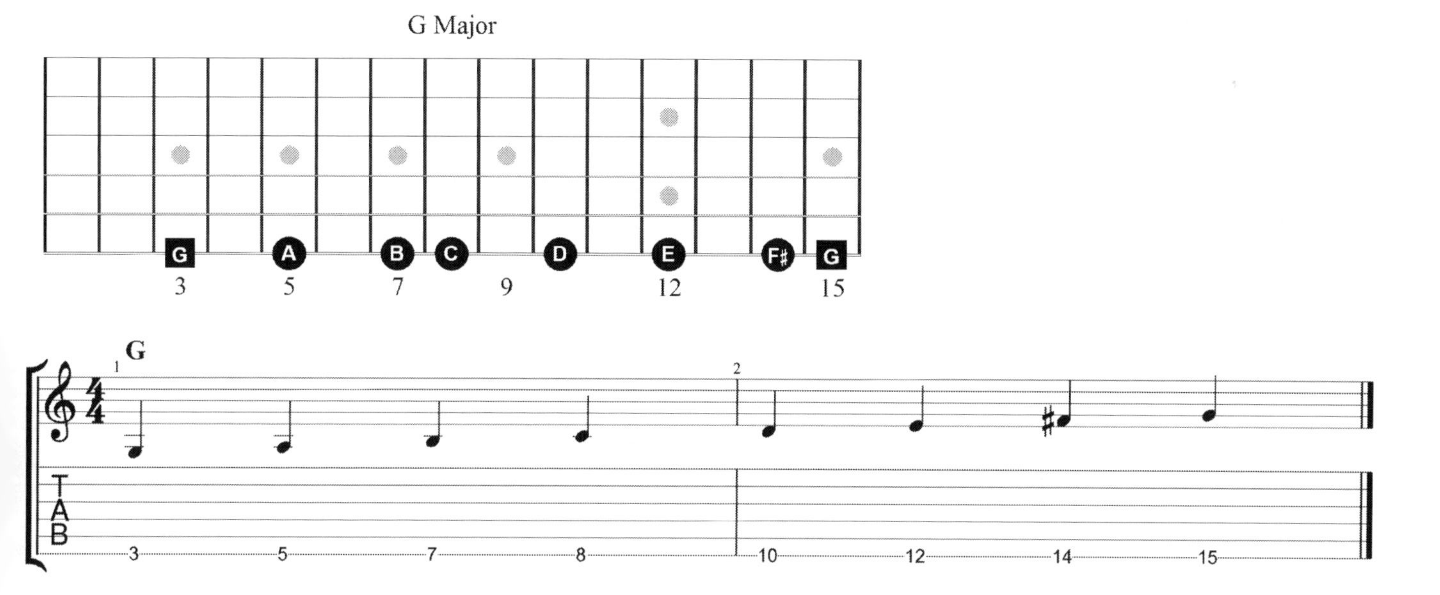

To create the correct Major scale pattern of **Tone, Tone, Semitone, Tone, Tone, Tone Semitone,** we had to raise the 7th note of the scale by one semitone.

This scale is now identical in construction to the C Major scale that we studied in the last chapter so it has the formula **1 2 3 4 5 6 7**

Before we raised the 7th note to F#, we would have described it as: **1 2 3 4 5 6 b7**

We needed to raise the 7th note to make it conform to the Major scale formula.

The Circle of 5ths

I did not choose the scale of G Major by chance. There's a rule in music that says, "If you ascend a Major scale five notes, and begin a new scale from that point, you must always sharpen the 7th note of the new scale to fit it to the Major scale formula."

That sounds complex on paper and it's a bit of a mouthful, so let's recap the previous example and look at a few others.

The second scale I tried to form was the scale of G Major. Beginning with the scale of C Major, I ascended 5 notes. C, D, E, F, **G**

From the 5th note, G, I formed a new scale, *using all the notes* from the previous major scale of C:

G A B C D E F G.

I then sharpened (or raised) the 7th note of the new scale to make it match the formula for a Major scale.

G A B C D E F# G

This is now the correct scale of G Major, because it obeys the pattern **Tone, Tone, Semitone, Tone, Tone, Tone Semitone.**

Let's study the next example:

The previous scale was G Major. Ascend 5 notes; G A B C **D.**

Form a new scale from D and *include all the notes* from the previous scale:

D E F# G A B C D

Sharpen the 7th note:

D E F# G A B C# D

This now forms the correct scale of D Major. As you can see, it follows the set pattern of tones and semitones and has the same 1 2 3 4 5 6 7 formula as the C Major scale. Remember, we simply shift our ladder to a different note.

Example 3c:

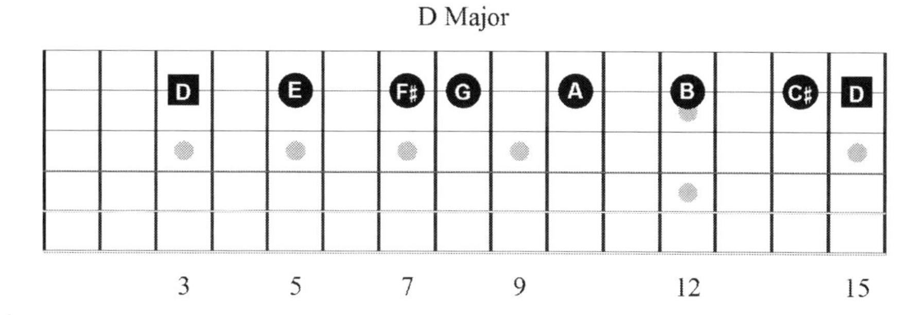

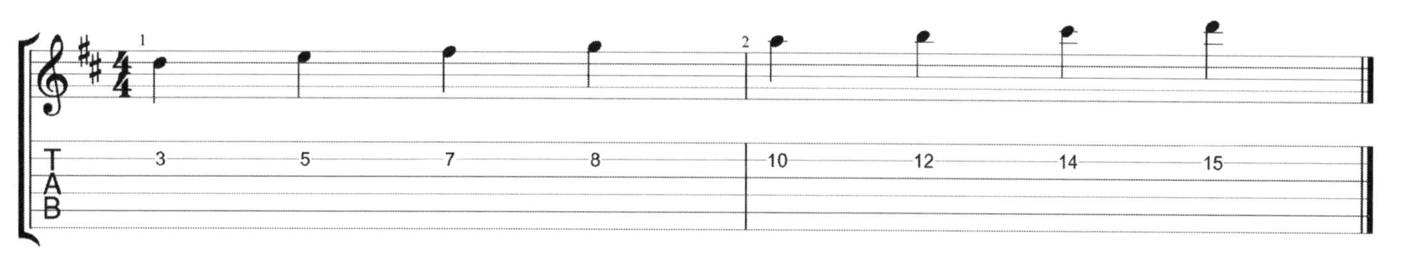

Play through this example so you can hear that the scale is correct.

Let's repeat this process one more time:

The previous scale was D Major. Ascend 5 notes; D E F# G **A**

Form a new scale from A and include all the notes from the previous scale:

A B C# D E F# G A

Sharpen the 7th note:

A B C# D E F# **G#** A

We have now formed the scale of A Major. Test it in the same way to make sure it is correct.

Following this rule, we can form all 'sharp key' Major scales. This rule is called 'The Circle of Fifths' because of how you always form a new scale from the fifth note of the previous one.

I've written a whole book about the **circle of fifths**. It's sold thousands of copies and goes into a massive amount of detail on the whole concept.

Playing the Major Scale in One Position

Until now, we have spread out the notes of the Major scale along one string so we can see the steps in a linear fashion. As guitarists, however, we often like to play scales in one position on the neck so they all fit nicely underneath our fingers.

The following scale shape is the *root position* of the C Major scale. Root position means that the lowest note of the scale, (C) is the first note that we play in the shape. The following scale shape covers *two* octaves, not just one as we have been discussing so far.

Example 4a:

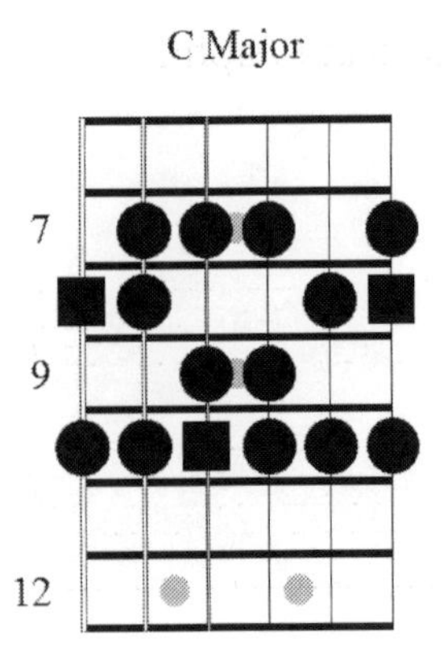

The squared dots are the roots of the scale.

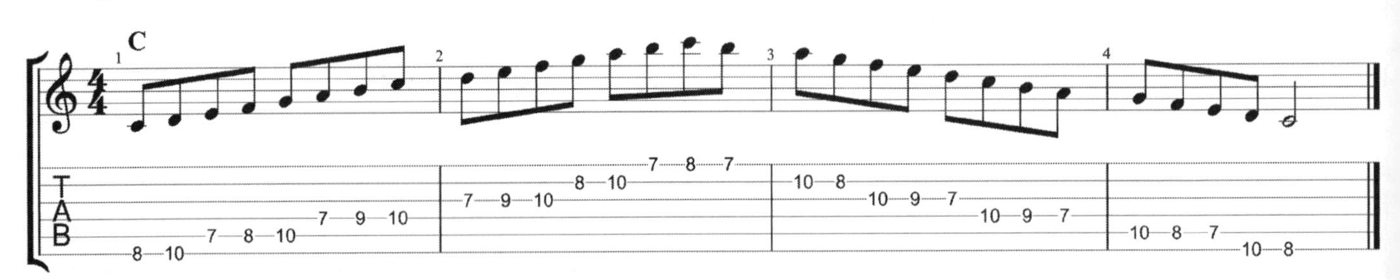

Play through this example *slowly*. The objective is to *hear* and understand how this scale sounds and functions musically. Remember, all the audio examples in this book are available from **www.fundamental-changes.com.**

It is vital that you spend time memorising this scale pattern. There is no point knowing theory without knowing how it sounds and how to use it.

To help you memorise this scale, try to visualise it being played through a C Major barre chord shape:

Example 4b:

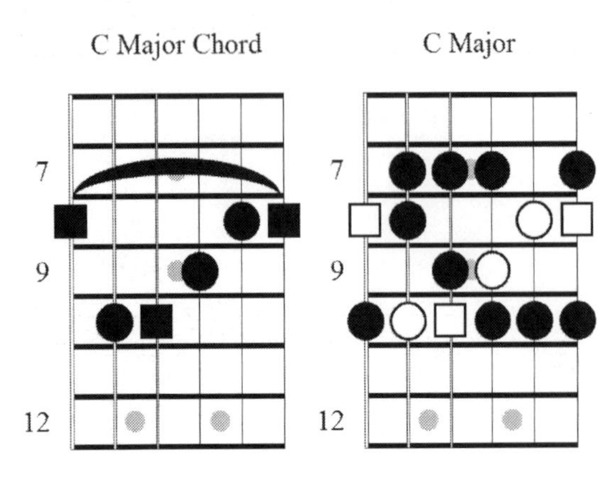

In this book, useful chord shapes will always be highlighted by hollow dots on each scale diagram.

Once you have memorised the scale shape, play it ascending and descending in 1/16th notes at 80bpm.

Example 4c:

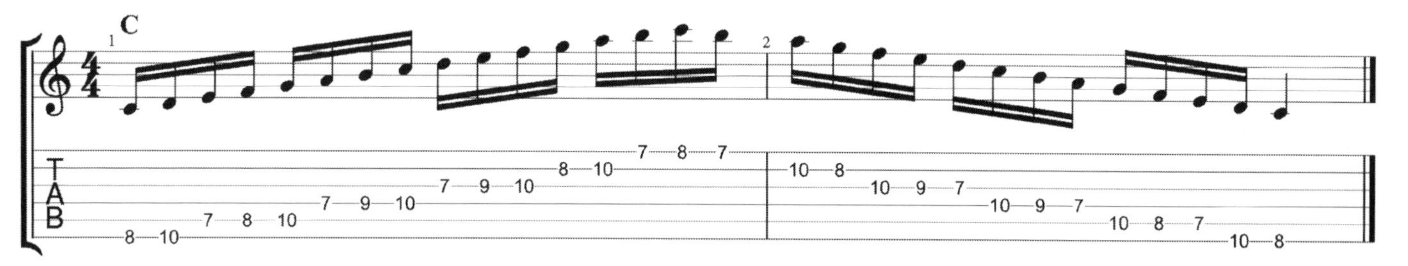

My bestselling guitar book, **Complete Technique for Modern Guitar**, teaches how to develop technique, increase speed and improve fluency with all of the common scale shapes.

In the second part of this book we will look at how to use the Major scale to create musical solos.

Key Signatures

One easy way to tell which *key* a piece of music is in is to look at the number of sharps at the beginning of the music. This is called a *key signature.* You will remember that C Major contained no sharps or flats, therefore, the key signature of C Major contains no sharps or flats:

However, the scale of G Major contained the note F#, so the key signature for G Major shows an F#:

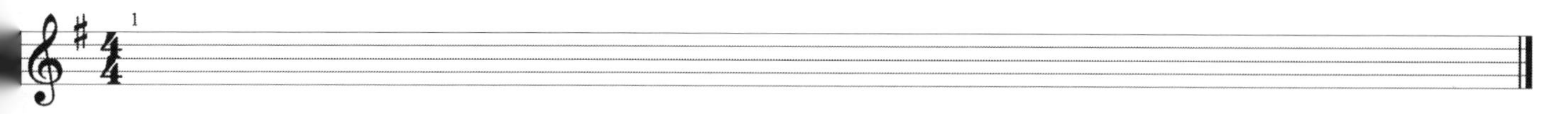

D Major contained the notes F# and C#:

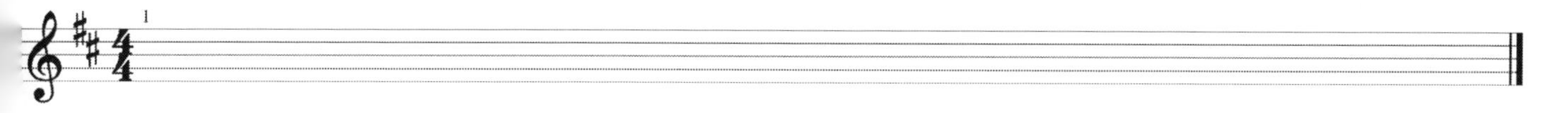

And A Major contained F# C# and G#:

If you want to quickly tell which key the music is written in, look at the final sharp on the right of the key signature, and go up a semitone. For example, in the key of D Major, the final sharp on the right is C# (the 7th that we raised when we formed the scale). One semitone up from C# = D Major.

If the last sharp in the key signature is G#, you are in A Major.

If the last sharp in the key signature is D#, you are in E Major.

The following table shows the order of keys, and number of sharps you generate when you follow the circle of fifths as described above:

Key	Order of Sharps	Number of Sharps
C Major	/	0
G Major	F#	1
D Major	F#, C#	2
A Major	F#, C#, G#	3
E Major	F#, C#, G#, D#	4
B Major	F#, C#, G#, D#, A#	5
F# Major	F#, C#, G#, D#, A#, E#	6

In music, there are two keys that share a key signature; one major key and one minor key.

Relative Minor Keys

It is important to address the idea of shared key signatures to prevent confusion before we move on.

Each major key has a closely related minor key. The purest form of the Minor scale shares identical notes to the Major scale; hence them having the same key signature. Often this *relative minor* scale is referred to as the *Natural Minor* or you may have heard it called *The Aeolian Mode*. They are the same thing.

To easily find the relative minor scale of any major scale, ascend six notes up the major scale and begin a new scale from there. Because we start on a different note, the patterns of tones and semitones throughout the minor scale are different to the major scale and therefore it will sound different.

For example, in the key of C Major, ascend six notes up the scale:

C D E F G **A**

A Minor is the relative Minor of C Major.

A B C D E F G

The key signature of A Minor is the same as that of C Major and contains no sharps or flats.

In G:

G A B C D **E**

E Minor is the relative Minor of G Major.

The key signature of E Minor is the same as that of G Major and contains one sharp, (F#).

E F# G A B C D

Natural Minor Construction

When we form a new scale from the sixth note of the Major scale, it has a new pattern of tones and semitones.

Tone, Semitone, Tone, Tone, Semitone, Tone, Tone. This can be seen easily in the following diagram.

Example 4d:

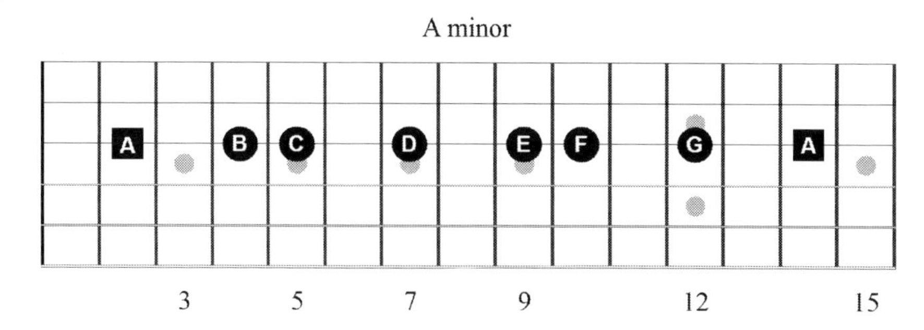

Compared to the Major scale, the formula for the natural Minor scale is

1 2 b3 4 5 b6 b7

A quick way to see this, is that there are only three semitones (a *Minor* 3rd) between the first and third notes.

You can also see that the 7th note of the scale, G (12th fret) is one tone below the root of 'A'. When the 7th note is one tone below the root, it is *always* a b7.

The b6 is harder to see, but examine the A *Major* scale shown earlier and you will see that the sixth note is F#. Here it is F natural and has therefore been flattened.

If we compare the scale of A Natural Minor with the scale of A Major it is easy to see the alterations.

A Major: A B C# D E F# G# (1 2 3 4 5 6 7)

A Minor: A B C D E F G (1 2 b3 4 5 b6 b7)

The other types of minor scale you may come across are the *Harmonic Minor* and *Melodic Minor.* These scales are based on the natural Minor (or Aeolian mode), but with the alteration of certain scale degrees.

The *Harmonic Minor* scale has the formula:

1 2 b3 4 5 b6 7 (The 7th degree is raised a semitone from the Natural Minor). In the key of A, that formula gives A B C D E F G#

The *Melodic Minor* scale has the formula:

1 2 b3 4 5 6 7 (This is often viewed by guitarists as simply the Major scale with a flattened 3rd). In the key of A, that formula gives A B C D E F# G#

The Natural Minor scale is covered in more detail in later chapters, so for now let's continue our focus on major scale theory.

Harmonising the Major Scale

When we use the word 'harmonising', what we mean is 'building chords'. When we harmonise the Major scale, we build a three-note chord on each note of the scale.

What is a chord?

A chord, technically, is the combination of three or more notes. A pure Major or Minor chord has only three individual notes. When we strum Major or Minor chords on the guitar we normally play more than three strings. Even though we play major and minor chords on four, five, or even six strings, we actually only play three individual notes that are doubled in different octaves.

For example, in the following chord of C Major the names of the notes are labelled… You can see that even though we play six strings, there are only three unique notes.

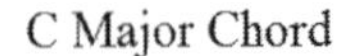
C Major Chord

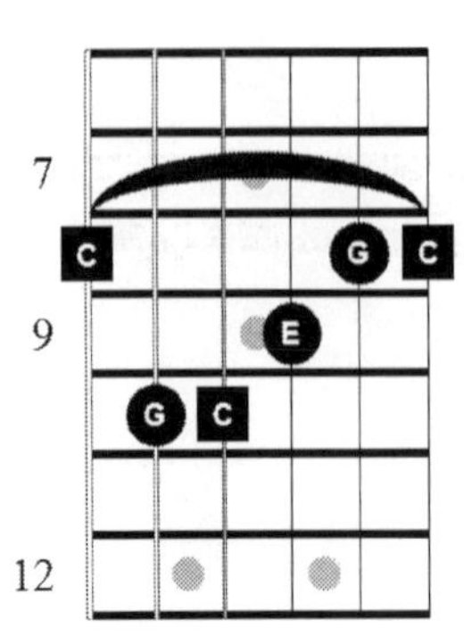

In this voicing, the note C appears three times, and the note G appears twice. The only note to appear once is the E.

Where do these notes come from?

Chords are formed when we 'stack' certain notes from a scale on top of each other. Look again at the previous example. The chord of C Major contains only the notes, C, E and G. In the context of the Major scale formula, we have taken the notes 1, 3 and 5:

C	D	E	F	G	A	B	C
1	2	3	4	5	6	7	8/1

This process of 'leapfrogging' every other note in the scale is the most common way to form chords and is an essential concept in *harmonisation*. For example, we formed this chord by beginning on C, jumping D to land on E, then jumping F to land on G. This is how most simple, three-note chords are formed.

In the C Major scale, we can generate the following chords by harmonising each note of the scale:

C E G

D F A

E G B

F A C

G B D

A C E

B D F

When we view the notes of C Major spaced out on the fretboard, we discover what pattern of notes is required to form a *Major* chord. Remember, Major and Minor scales and chords all have a set formula. A chord type will always have the same formula, even if the notes are different.

Example 5a:

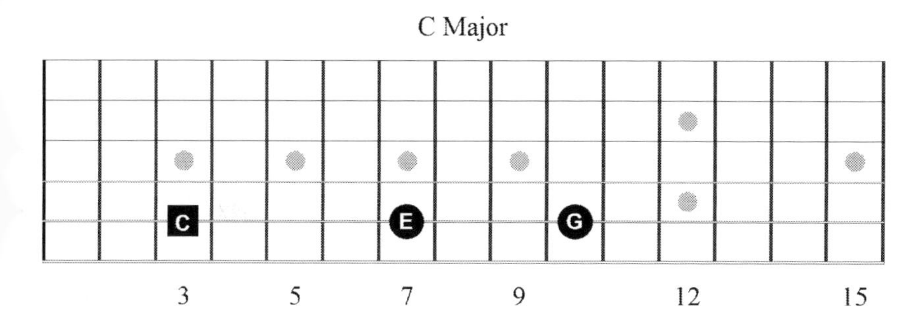

The distance between the notes C and E is *two tones*.

Any chord with two tones between the first two notes is classed as a Major type chord. This two-tone distance in music is called a *major 3rd.*

The distance between the 3rd and 5th (the notes E and G), is *one-and-a-half tones*. This is *one semitone smaller* than the major 3rd so we call it a *minor* 3rd.

When measured from the *root*, any major chord *must* consist of two tones between the root and 3rd, and three-and-a-half tones between the root and 5th. A three-and-a-half-tone distance is called a *perfect 5th.* Over 95% of all chords, including Major, Minor and Dominant 7 chords contain a perfect 5th.

It is convention in music to describe the notes in a chord in terms of their relationship to the Major scale formula, **1 2 3 4 5 6 7**.

In simple terms a major chord has the formula 1 3 5 and **the first chord in any major key is always major.**

Moving on to the second note in the C Major scale, (D) and repeating the previous process we generate the notes:

C	D	E	F	G	A	B	C
1	2	3	4	5	6	7	8/1

When we harmonise the second note of the scale, we generate the notes D, F and A. On the guitar, that looks and sounds like this:

Example 5b:

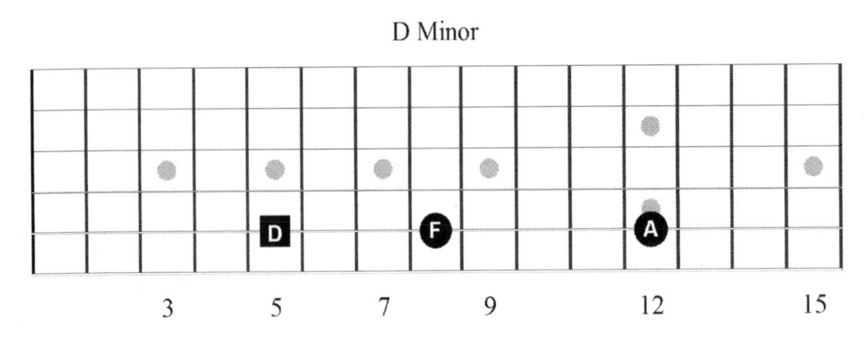

The distance between the first two notes, D and F is one-and-a-half tones or a *minor 3rd.* This means that the chord is *minor*.

The distance between the notes D and A is still three-and-a-half tones, which is the correct spacing for a *perfec* 5th.

With a minor 3rd and a perfect 5th, this is a Minor chord built on the note D, or simply 'D Minor' for short.

A Minor chord's formula is written as 1 b3 5 and **the second chord in any major key is always minor.**

All the notes of the Major scale can be harmonised in this way, and except for the 7th note they are all Major or Minor chords.

To save space I will not show the construction of every chord (although do try this by yourself). The harmonised chords of the C Major scale are:

Chord 1 (I)	C Major
Chord 2 (ii)	D Minor
Chord 3 (iii)	E Minor
Chord 4 (IV)	F Major
Chord 5 (V)	G Major
Chord 6 (vi)	A Minor
Chord 7 (vii)	B Minor (*b5*) or B *Diminished*

Harmonising the 7th Degree of the Major Scale

The 7th or *leading note* in the Major scale is different. It is the only chord that does not contain a perfect fifth. When we harmonise the 7th degree of a Major scale, the 5th is only three tones which is one semitone smaller than a perfect 5th called a *diminished 5th*, or b5 for short. The 7th note in the scale of C Major is B.

This can be heard in **example 5c:**

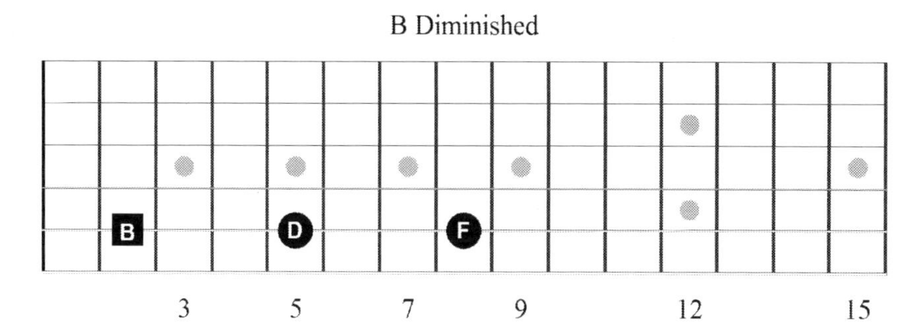

The distance between the notes B and D is a Minor 3rd so this must be some type of Minor chord. However, the distance between the notes B and F is only six semitones, not seven as in the previous examples. This chord is therefore named B Minor(b5) or B *Diminished.* Try playing it.

Example 5d:

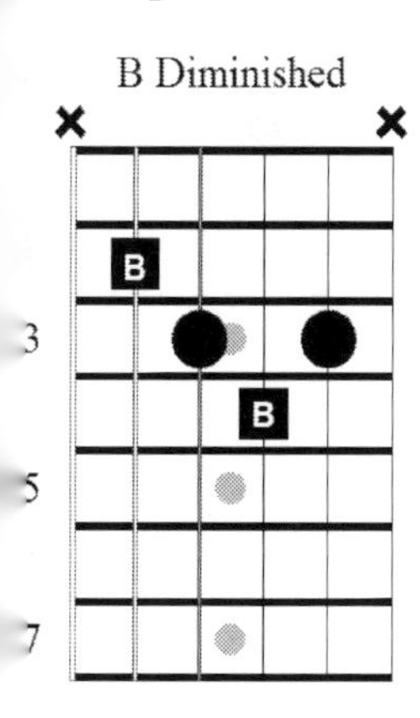

This is the only chord in Major scale harmony that does not contain a perfect 5th. It is not often used in pop music due to its *dissonant* nature. When it is used, it is normally a *substitution* for the 5th chord in the scale.

The Roman Numeral System

In music, chords are often referred to by the Roman numeral numbering system. Instead of labelling them 1, 2, 3, 4, 5, etc., they are given the Roman numeral equivalent numbers.

1 = I, 2 = ii, 3 = iii, 4 = IV, 5 = V, 6 = vi, 7 = vii.

This is to avoid confusion when we're talking about intervals. Intervals are given the names 3rds, 4ths and 5ths, and chords are given the names iii, IV or V

You will notice that sometimes I've used capital letters and sometimes lower case letters for each numeral. Capital letters are used to describe Major chords and lower case letters to describe Minor chords.

You can see that in a major key, chords I, IV and V are always Major chords, whereas ii, iii, vi and vii are Minor.

Playing the Chords of the Harmonised C Major Scale

Now we have harmonised all the notes of the C Major scale, you can play them in the open position.

Examples 6a – 6g:

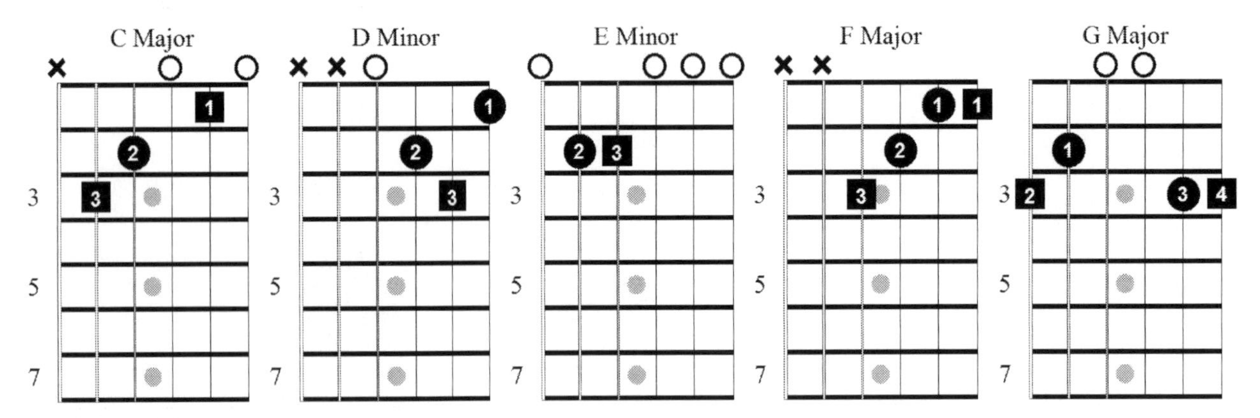

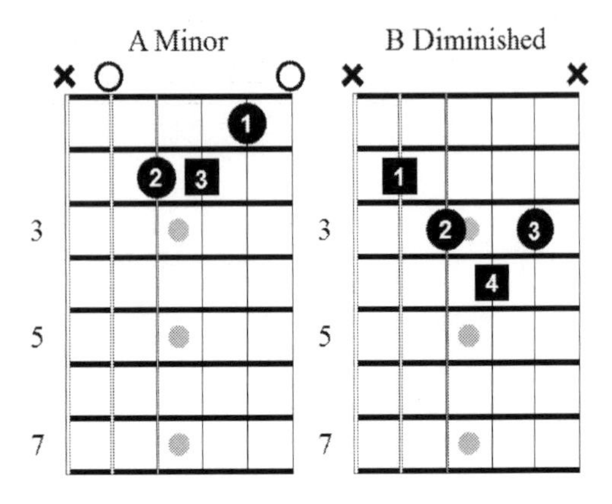

Common Chord Progressions from the Major Scale

Now you know how to form the basic chords of the Major scale, it is important to you play them and learn how they function in modern music. While there are no rights or wrongs when writing music, there are some great standard chord sequences to learn before you start to break the rules.

Chord progressions, as mentioned before, are normally described in terms of Roman numerals.

To recap each chord of the Major scale look at the following table:

Chord 1 (I)	C Major
Chord 2 (ii)	D Minor
Chord 3 (iii)	E Minor
Chord 4 (IV)	F Major
Chord 5 (V)	G Major
Chord 6 (vi)	A Minor
Chord 7 (vii)	B Minor (b5) or B *Diminished*

In this section I will give each example chord progression as both a chord chart and a *formula* which you can use to *transpose* the chord progression into different keys.

The progression shown in example 7a is probably the most common chord progression in western music.

The structure of the progression is I, IV, V, IV.

Example 7a:

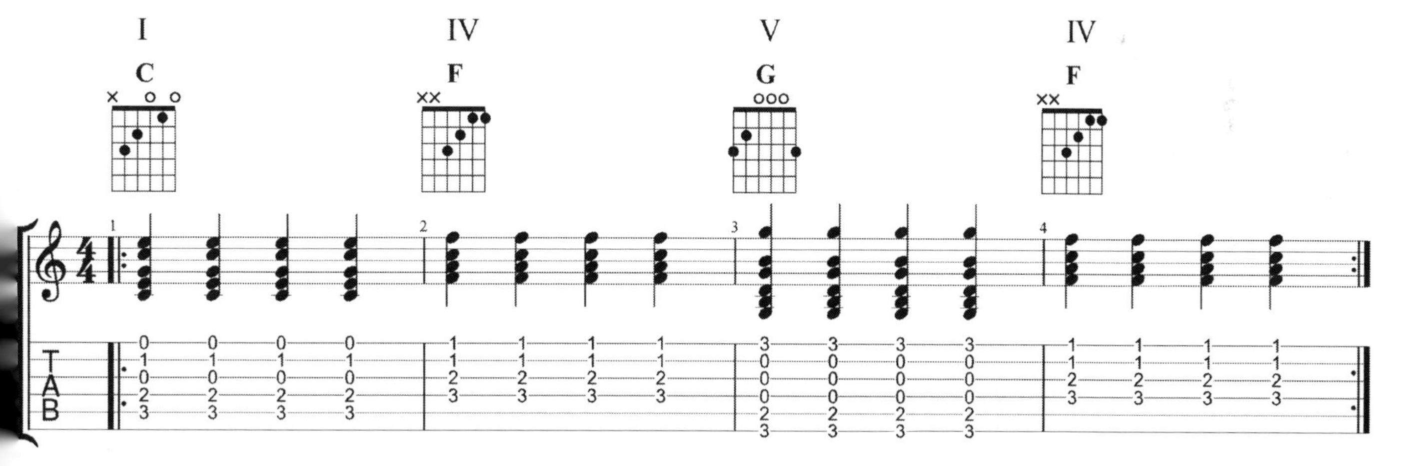

Example 7b shows the chord progression I, vi, ii, V. Again, this is an extremely common progression in popular music.

Example 7b:

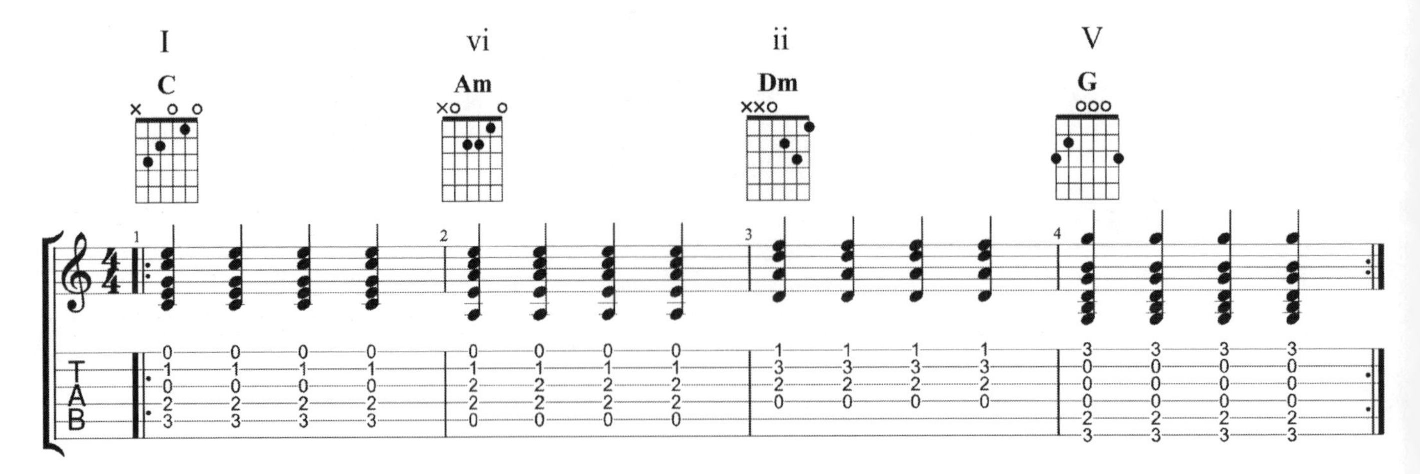

I, IV, ii, V is something you will have heard in many songs.

Example 7c:

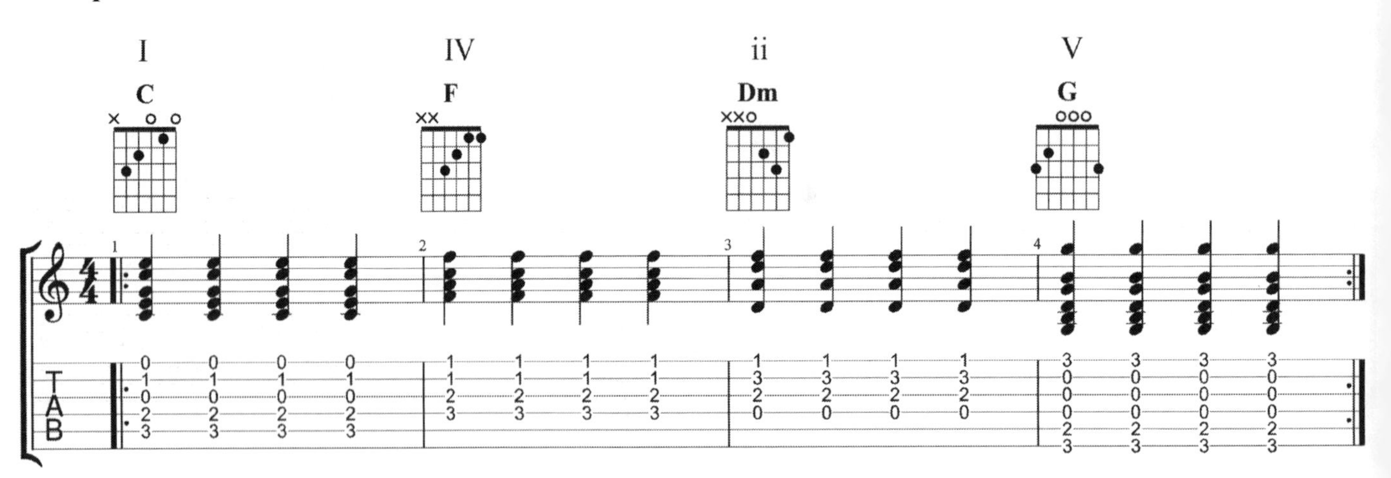

Chord progressions don't have to start on chord I. Here are some useful ideas that begin on other degrees of the scale.

The vi, IV, I, V, progression:

Example 7d:

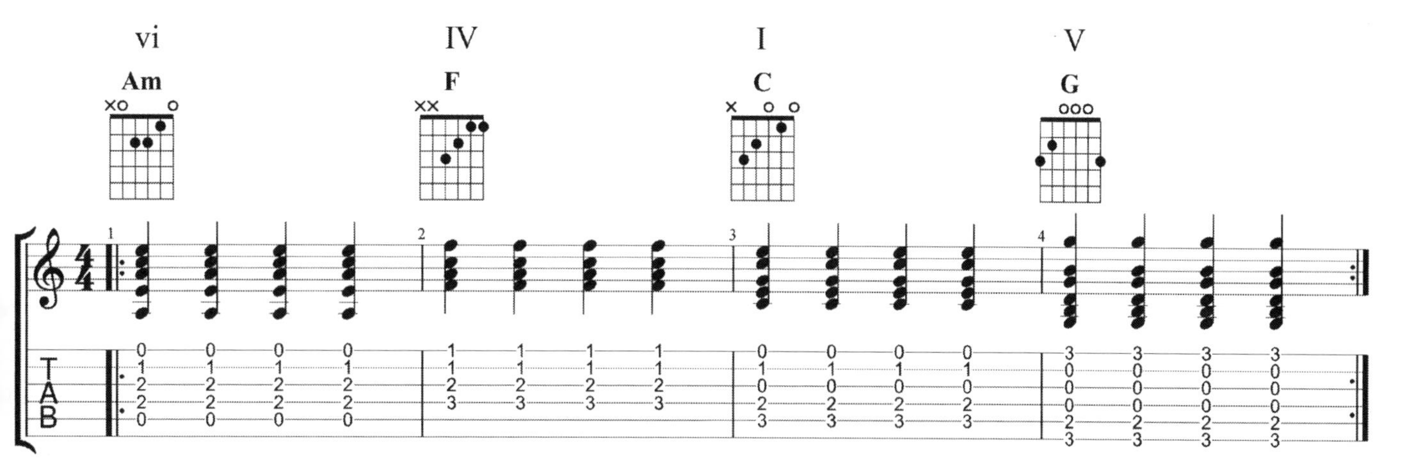

Others you might hear are IV, V, iii, vi:

Example 7e:

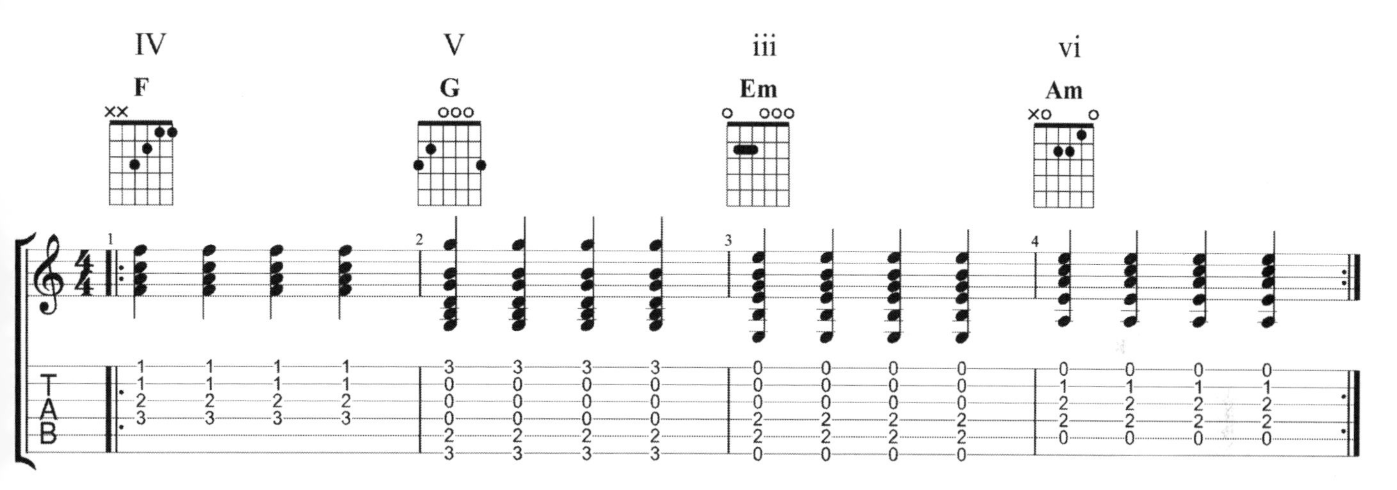

Or ii, iii, IV, V:

Example 7f:

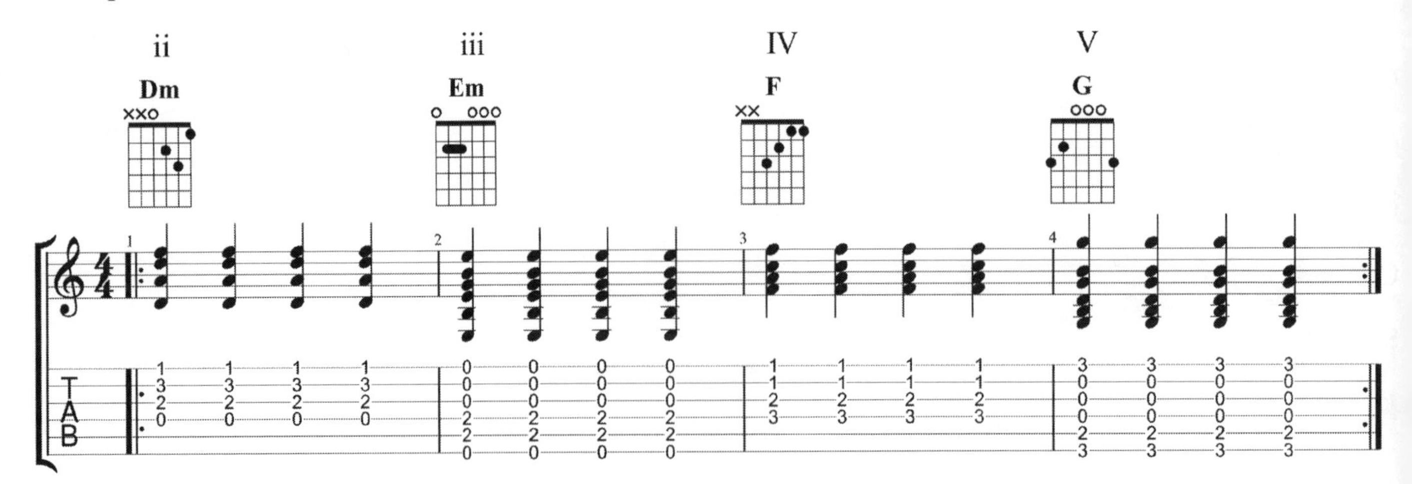

There are many possible permutations of chord progressions and some sound stronger than others. The best thing is to get creative and write your own. Write a four-bar chord progression using just the chords in C Major. Listen to the chord progressions in the music you like and try to figure them out with just your guitar.

When you have developed this awareness you'll realise that certain chord progressions come up time and time again and it's simply the arrangement or *orchestration* of the chords that disguises these common sequences.

Transposing Chord Progressions into Other Keys

As we have seen, common chord progressions often follow set formulas. This means that it is easy to *transpose* a chord progression into another key once we have worked out how each chord fits into the Roman numeral system. For example, take the following chord progression in the key of C Major:

Example 8a:

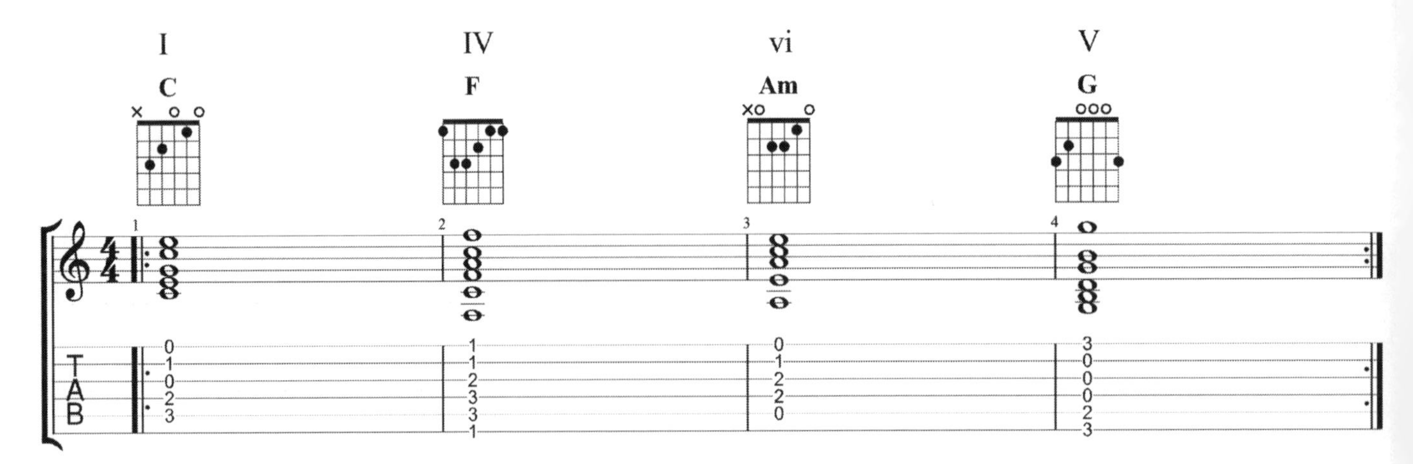

Analysing it with Roman numerals shows us that in the key of C we are playing

Chord I, Chord IV, Chord vi and Chord V.

We can now shift this progression into any other key by transferring the same Roman numeral sequence to a different Major scale. For example, let's move it to the key of A Major, **(A B C# D E F# G#)**

In A Major,

Chord I is A Major

Chord IV is D Major

Chord VI is F# Minor

Chord V is E Major

So the transposed progression becomes:

Example 8b:

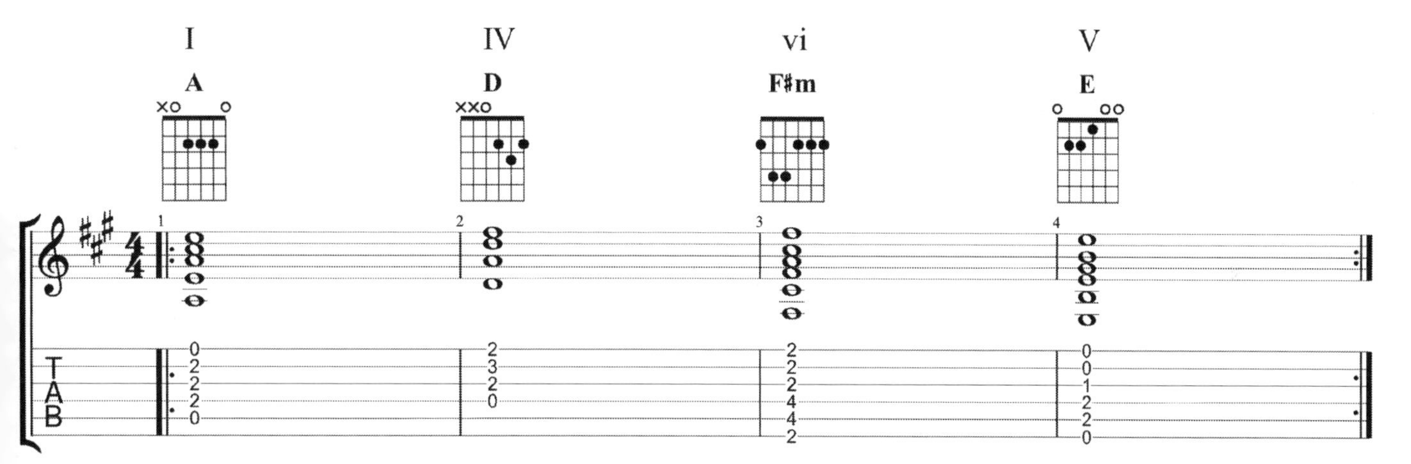

In the key of E, it becomes:

Example 8c:

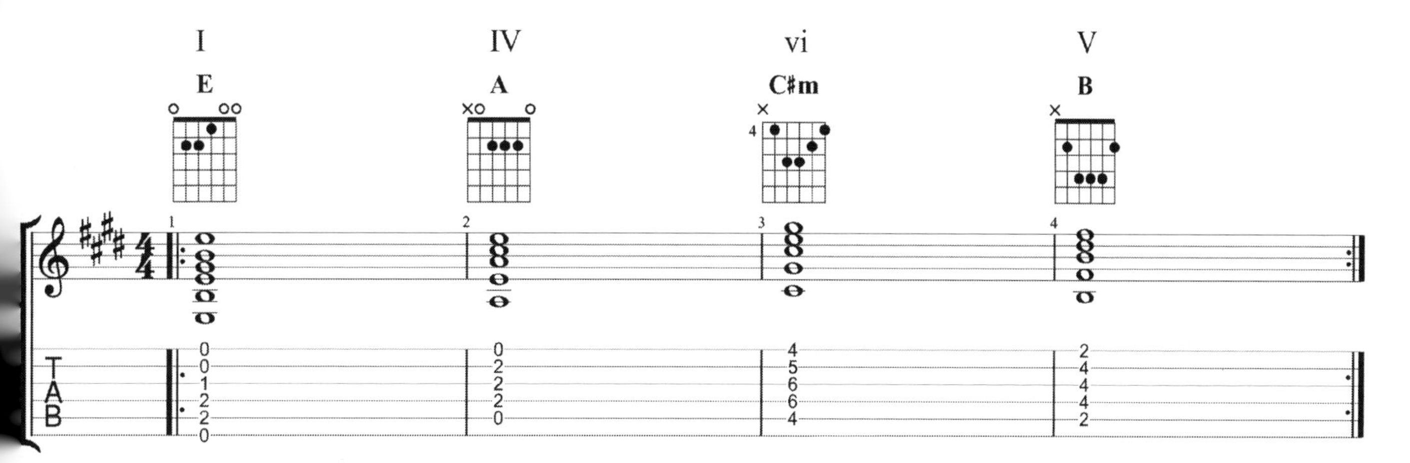

Write out the following two chord progressions in different keys.

a) I vi ii V

b) IV V I vi

Work out the Roman numerals for the following chord progressions in **G Major** and then transpose them to the key of **E Major.**

1)

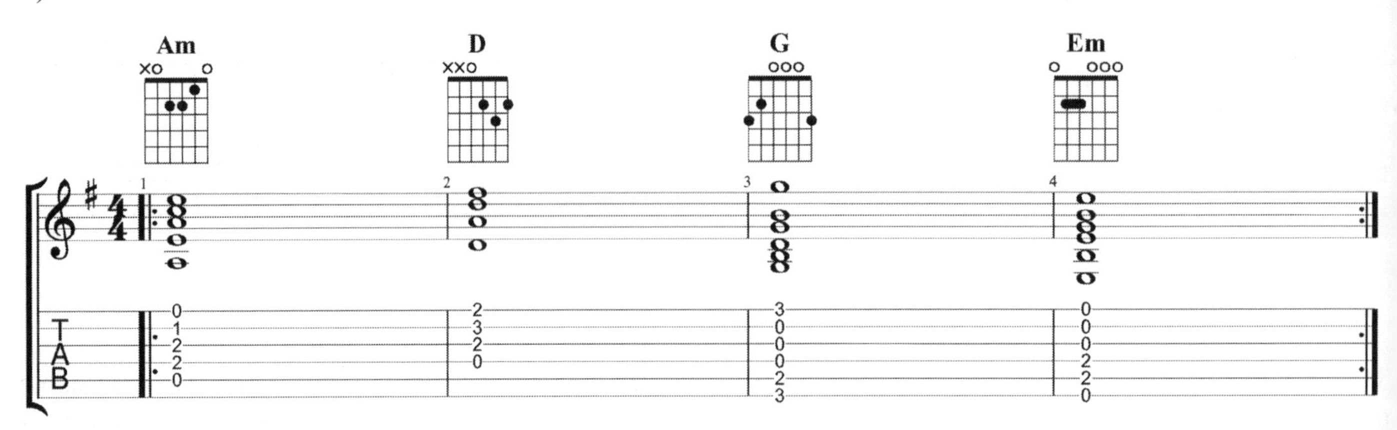

2)

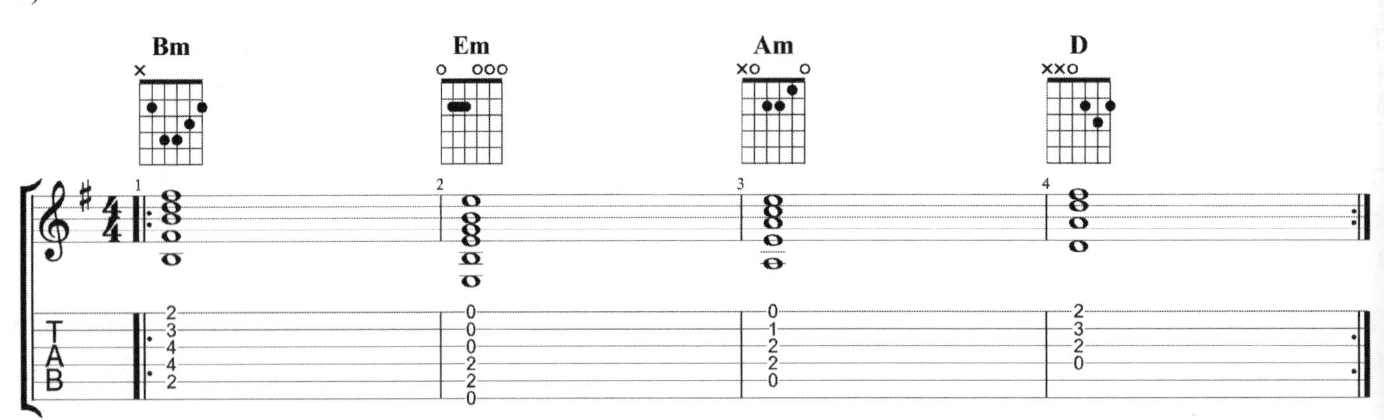

Practice transposition by analysing any song you are already familiar with, writing it out in Roman numerals and then moving those numerals into another key.

Chords from Outside the Key

Study the following chord progression:

Example 8d:

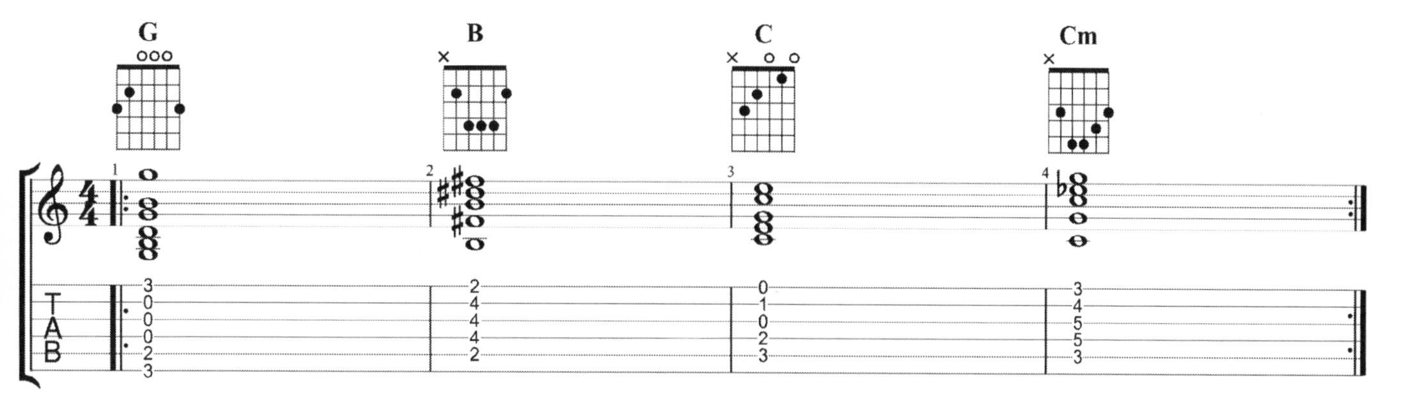

This progression is based on *Creep* by Radiohead and is in the key of G, however when we analyse it, we come across some chords that are not contained in the harmonised G Major scale. The second chord in the song is B *Major*. The note B is the third note in the key of G and as you might know by now, when we harmonise the third degree of a Major scale, we always form a *Minor* chord. Look at the table of harmonised chords earlier if you're not sure why the B chord in G Major should be Minor.

It is clear that the B Minor chord has been altered to become a B Major chord. This is perfectly fine to do, and happens all the time as alterations like this make the song much more interesting. So how do we write this in Roman numerals?

The B Major chord is still *functioning* as chord iii, but as it has been altered to become a Major chord instead of a Minor one, we simply write, 'III Major'. (Notice the capital *I's?* Lower case is for minor, upper case is for major).

The C Major in bar three is correct to the key (it is chord IV Major), but in bar four, the C Major becomes a C Minor chord. This would be written as 'iv minor'. Again, lower case numerals indicate that this is a Minor chord.

The full progression, therefore would be written as I, III(Major), IV, iv(Minor).

A Minor blues could be written

i(Minor), iv(Minor), v(Minor), i (Minor).

Example 8e:

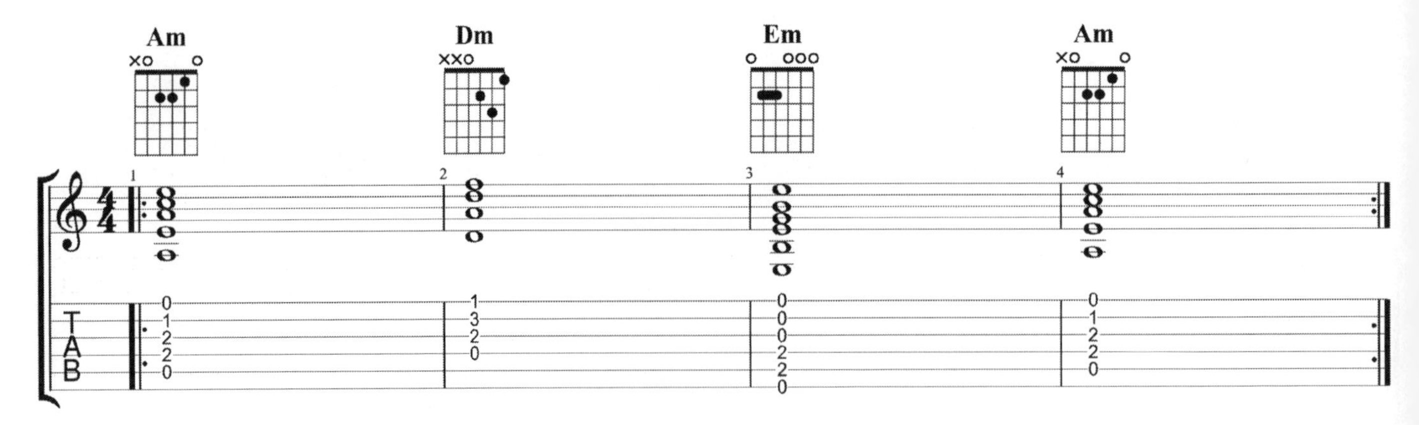

Sometimes, a chord may not even *exist* inside the scale of the parent key.

This chord progression comes from the middle section of *Sitting on the Dock of the Bay*, by Otis Redding. It is in the key of G.

Example 8f:

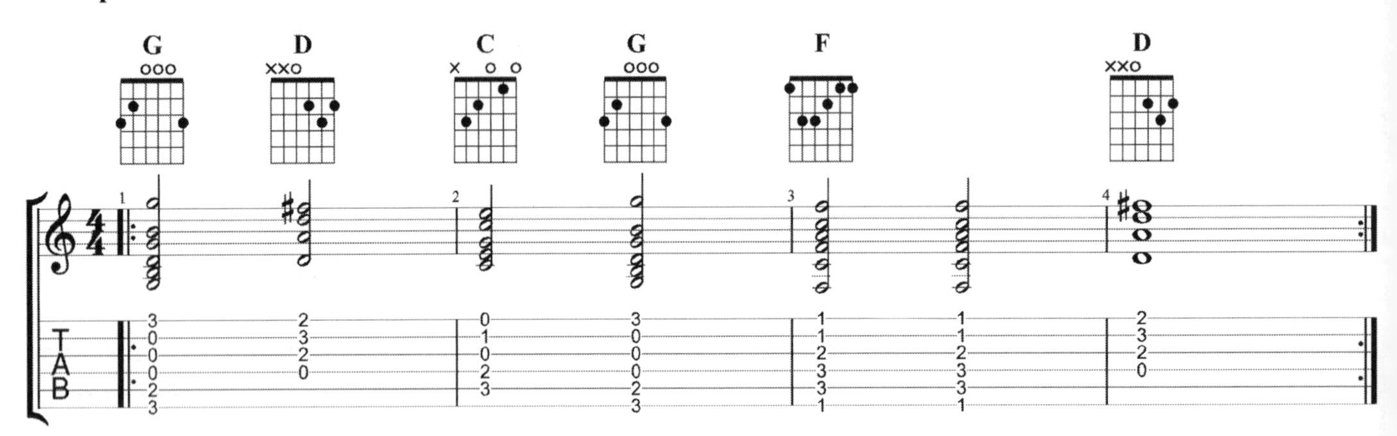

Each chord is derived from the harmonised scale of G Major, except for the F Major in bar three. The scale of G Major does not contain the note F (it should be F#).

In the Roman Numeral System, we notate the F Major by writing bVII (Major) because the 7th degree of the G Major scale (F#) has been *flattened* to become the note F, and is played as a Major chord.

The whole progression is I, V, IV, I, bVII (Major), V.

Another great use of the bVII (Major) is in the Blues Brothers song, *Everybody Needs Somebody.*

Example 8g:

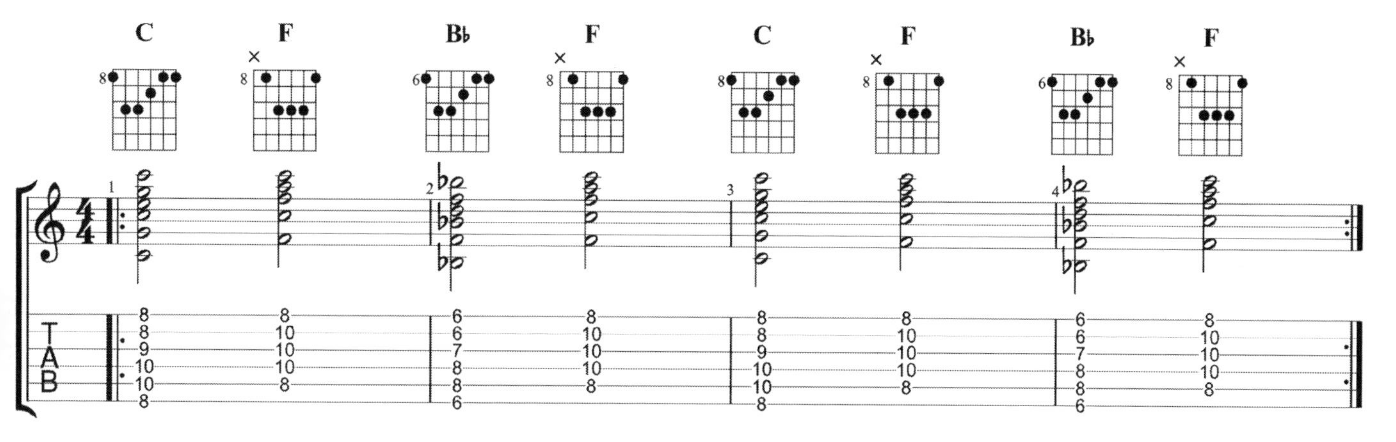

This progression is I, IV, bVII(Major), IV.

Another common *non-diatonic* chord is bIII(Major), used here in the key of A. In the key of A Major, you'd normally expect to see the chord C# Major. In the following example it is played as a C Major.

Example 8h:

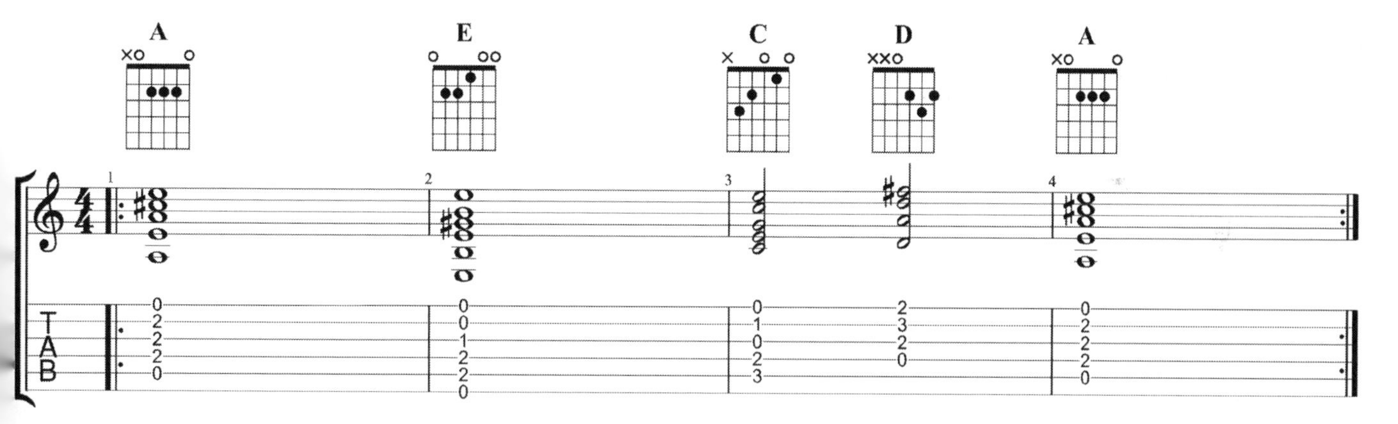

This progression is I, V, bIII(Major), IV, I.

A chord *The Beatles* used to good effect was bVI(Major). Here it is in the key of C:

Example 8i:

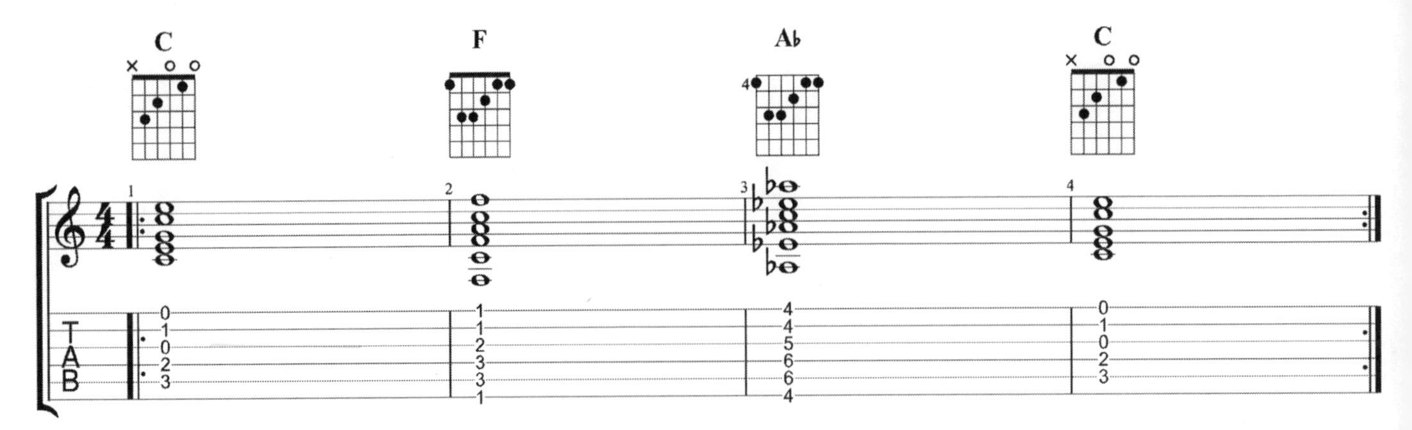

The progression is I, IV, bVI(Major), I.

Write these examples out in other keys, then make sure you can play and recognise them by ear.

7th Chords

In most modern music you will see chords with names like 'G7', 'A Minor 7', 'C Major 7' or even 'B Minor 7b5'. These chords are formed from the Major scale and are simply *extensions* of the original process we used to construct chords in the harmonisation section.

Look back at how we formed major and minor chords from the Major scale. We used the 1st, 3rd and 5th notes by leapfrogging adjacent scale tones. If we continue to jump notes and land on the 7 note, i.e., 1 3 5 **7** we create a 7th chord. For example:

C	D	E	F	G	A	B	C
1	2	3	4	5	6	7	8/1

Instead of just the notes C, E and G, we have now introduced the note B. This chord can be seen as a C Major *triad* with an added *natural 7th* and is named C Major 7, of CMaj7 for short. Notice how the 7th note, (B) is one semitone below the root, (C). The chord can be played like this:

Example 9a:

C Major 7

The added note, B is played on the open second string. Listen to this chord and notice how it has a richness when compared to an ordinary C Major chord.

The formua for a Major 7th chord is 1 3 5 7.

When we add the 7th note to chord ii in the key of C Major (D Minor), we get the following notes:

D F A C.

This time, the 7th note (C) is a *whole tone* below the root, (D). This 7th note is a *b7* not a *natural 7* as in the C Major 7th chord.

When we add a b7 note to a Minor chord, is becomes a Minor 7, or m7 for short. Here, we have formed the chord of D Minor 7

Example 9b:

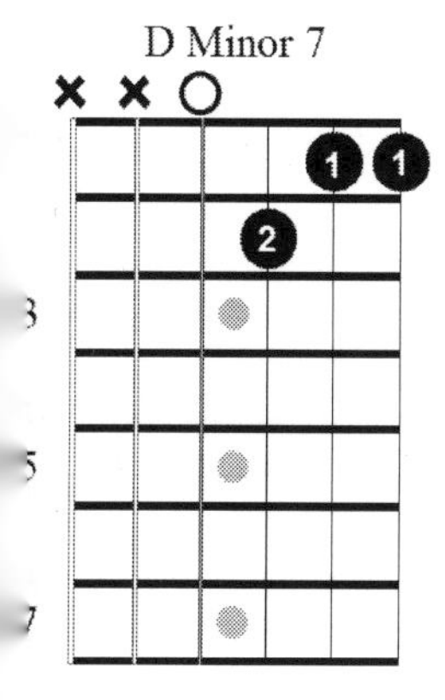

hear this as a *softened* minor chord. Still sad, but not as sad as a pure minor chord.

Any Minor 7 chord has the formual 1 b3 5 b7.

The previous two chord types, Major 7 and Minor 7, account for five of the harmonised Major scale chords.

Chord 1 (Imaj7)	C Major 7
Chord 2 (iim7)	D Minor 7
Chord 3 (iiim7)	E Minor 7
Chord 4 (IVmaj7)	F Major 7
Chord 5	
Chord 6 (vim7)	A Minor 7
Chord 7	

I have missed out chords V and vii because they are slightly different.

As you know from earlier, chord V of a Major scale is always a major chord. However, the added 7th note is *not* a natural 7th, it is a b7.

The harmonised V chord in the Key of C is G B D **F.**

The note F is a *whole tone* below the root, G, just like the b7th note in a Minor 7 chord. We have created a *major chord with an added b7.*

A Major chord with an added b7 is called a *dominant* 7 or simply '7'. E.g., *G7* or *A7.*

It has the formula 1 3 5 b7.

G7 can be played like this:

Example 9c:

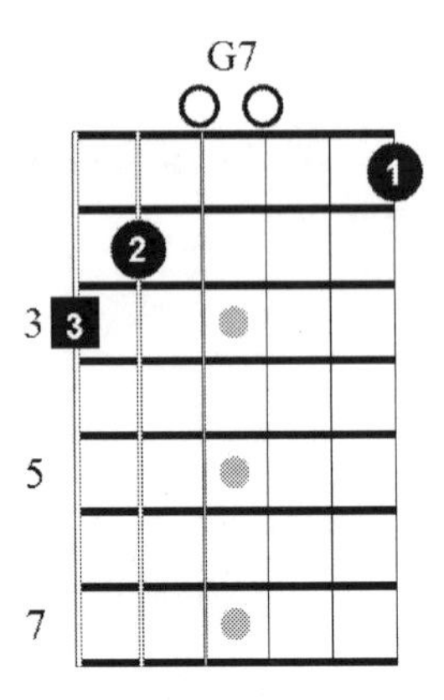

Dominant 7 chords have a tense, unresolved sound, and are often followed by chord I, in this case C Major.

When we harmonise the 7th note of the Major scale, we generate a chord which is rare in pop and rock music but common in jazz.

You learnt earlier that chord vii harmonises to become a *minor b5* chord. When we harmonise it up to four notes from the key of C, we get the notes B D F **A**

Again, we are adding a b7 to the original three-note structure and the chord can be named 'Minor 7b5' or *m7b5*. For example, the vii chord in C Major is Bm7b5. Any m7b5 chord has the formula 1 b3 b5 b7.

It is played like this and has a dark, brooding quality:

Example 9d:

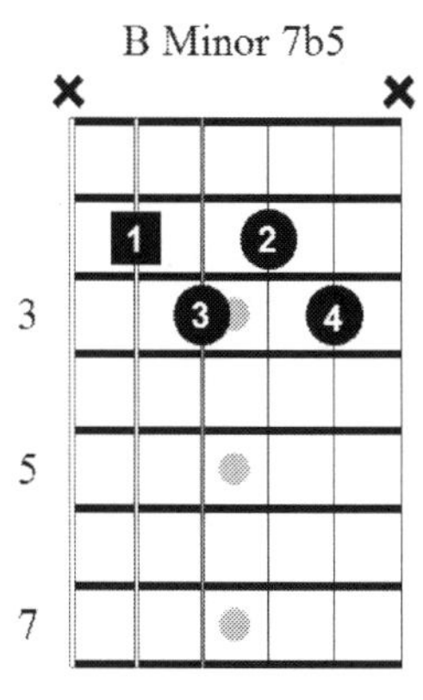

We can now complete the chord table for the harmonised Major scale.

Chord 1 (Imaj7)	C Major 7
Chord 2 (iim7)	D Minor 7
Chord 3 (iiim7)	E Minor 7
Chord 4 (IVmaj7)	F Major 7
Chord 5 (V7)	G7 or G *Dominant* 7
Chord 6 (vim7)	A Minor 7
Chord 7 (viim7b5)	B Minor 7 b5 or Bm7b5

7th chords can always be used to replace the three-note triads. There is no reason why the chord progression shouldn't be changed to:

Example 9e:

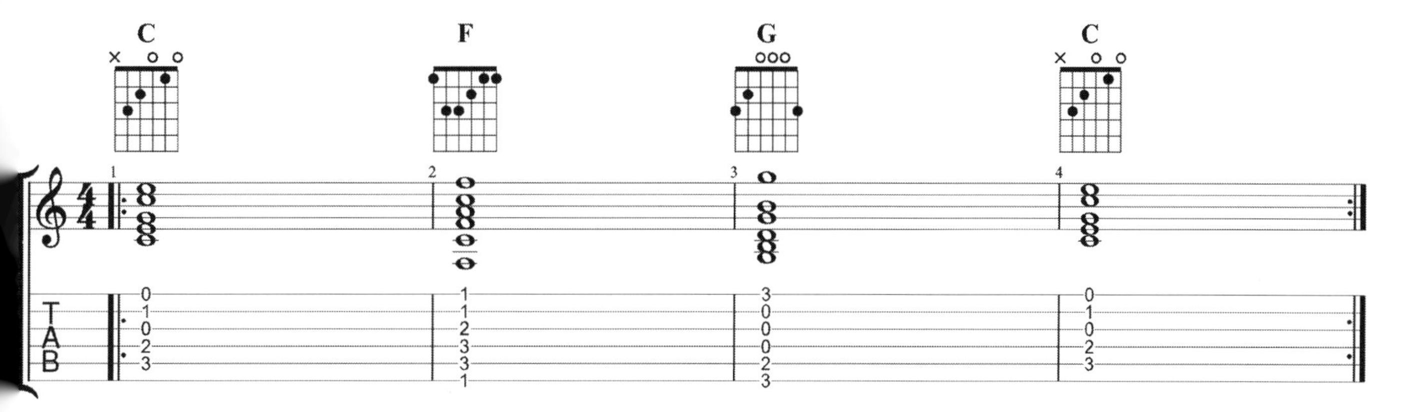

Example 9e part 2:

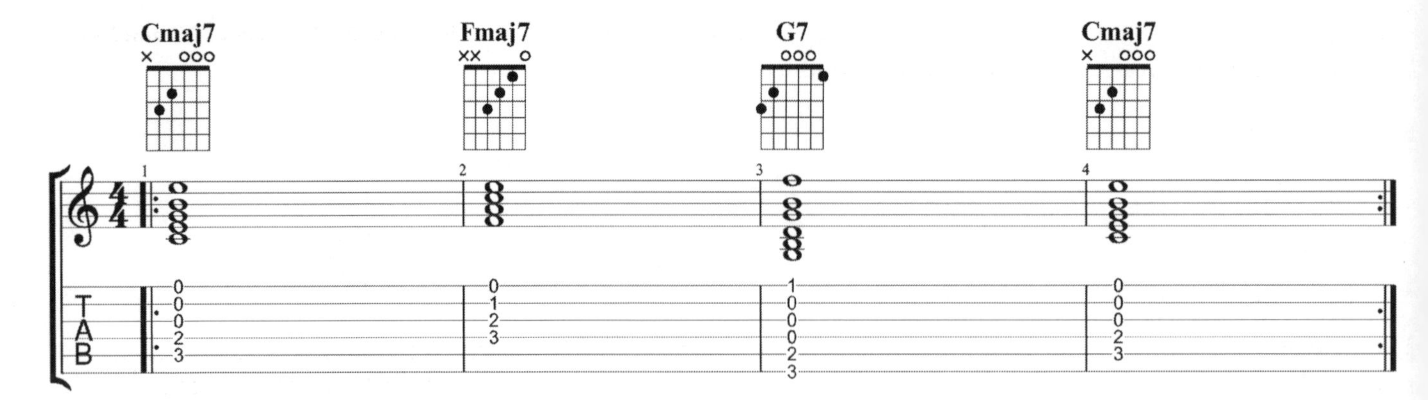

However, the added colour of the 7th note on a Major chord can be a bit too rich in most forms of pop music although they are used almost exclusively in jazz.

There are some great examples of Major 7th chords in rock music. Check out the F Major 7 in the fifth bar of this famous sequence

Example 9f:

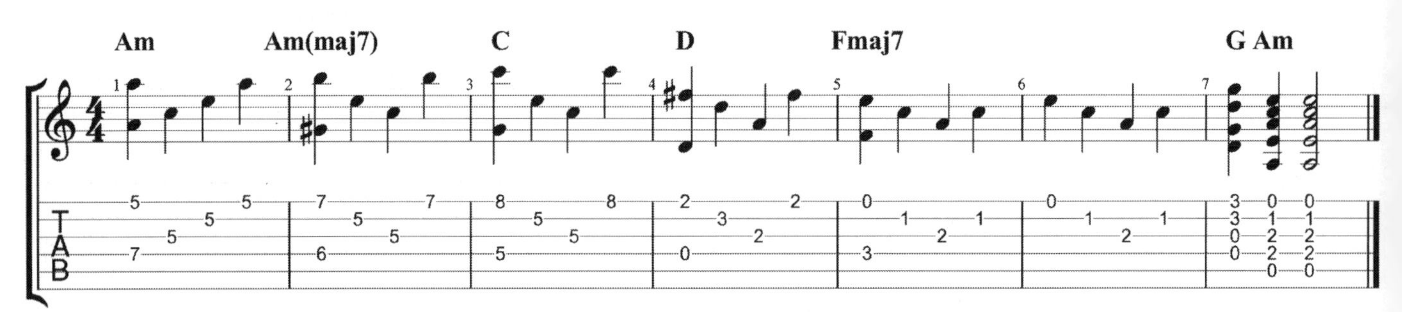

Another good example of a Major 7th chord in rock is at 0:53 in *Under the Bridge* by the Red Hot Chili Peppers

Dominant 7 chords are used all the time and can be used in place of every chord in the Major scale. For example compare example 9g to example 9e part 2:

Example 9g:

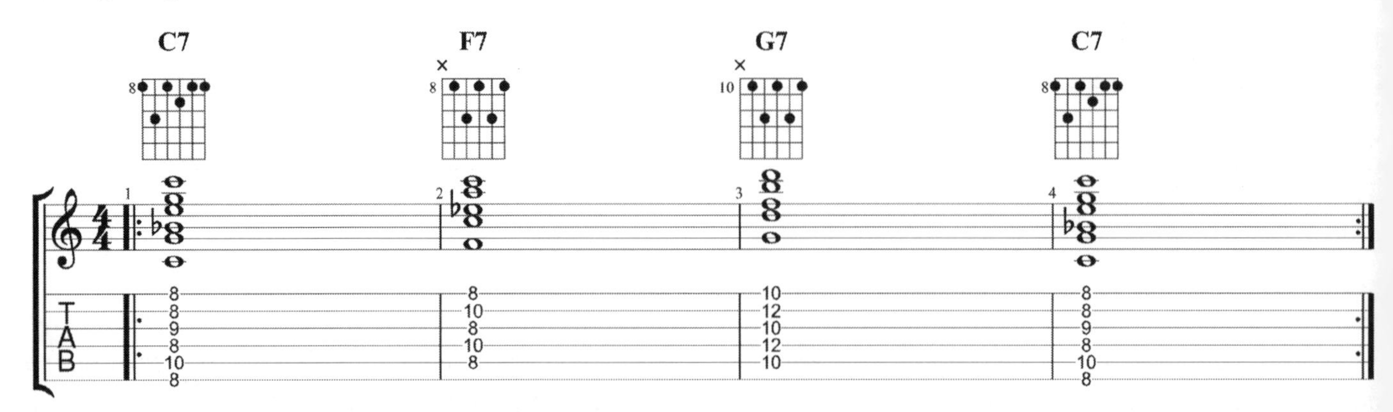

By making all the original chords into 7 chords the music sounds more bluesy.

When you use a dominant 7 chord in its context, i.e., as chord V in a Major key, it strongly pulls the music back to the I chord. Compare the following two examples:

Example 9h:

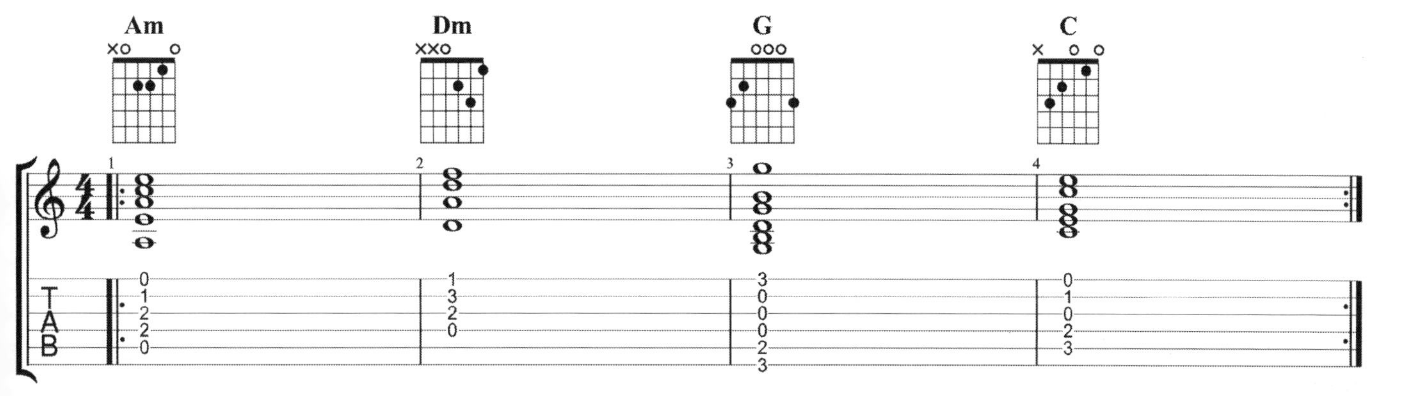

Example 9h (part 2):

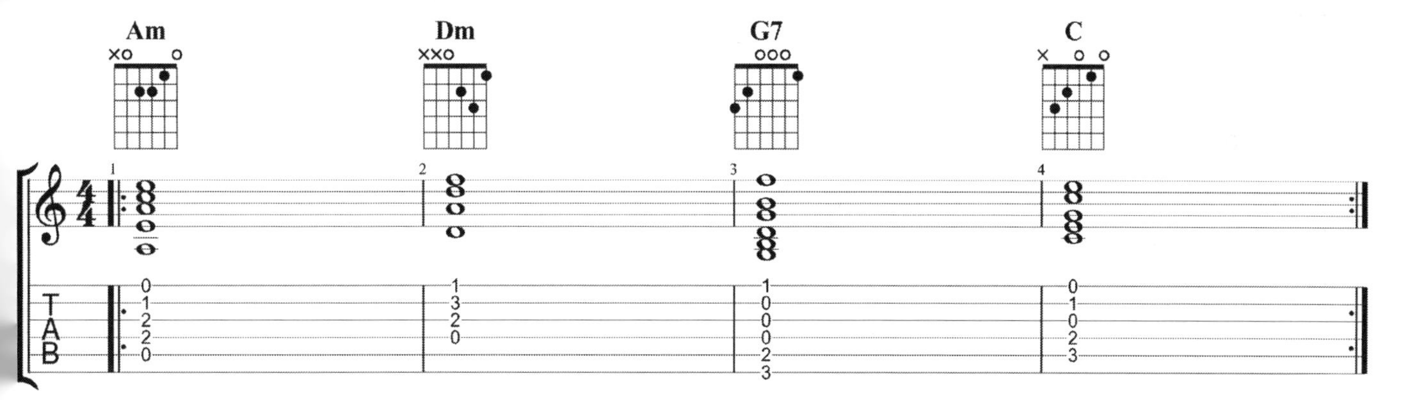

Listen to how the G7 in the second example adds more tension to the G Major chord and pulls more strongly back to the home chord of C Major.

Extensions

Extensions occur when we add notes from above the first octave of the scale to a 7th chord. For example, study the following:

C Major Scale	C	D	E	F	G	A	B	C	D	E	F	G	A	B
Interval Name	1	2	3	4	5	6	7	1	2/9	3	4/11	5	6/13	7

In the second octave, some notes have different interval names.

If a note is a chord tone, i.e. 1 3 5 or 7, the names do not change in the higher octave. This is because adding a chord tone in a different octave does not affect the *quality* of the chord. In other words, a Minor 7th chord that contains two b3rds still has the same fundamental characteristic as a Minor 7th chord with only one b3.

However, if you add a non-chord tone to the original 7th chord, it adds a different character or tension to the chord, and is therefore treated as an *extension*. Instead of being called 2, 4, or 6, they are named 9, 11, or 13.

For example, if you take an A Minor 7 chord, and add the 2nd/9th note, (B) it becomes an A Minor 9.

Example 9i:

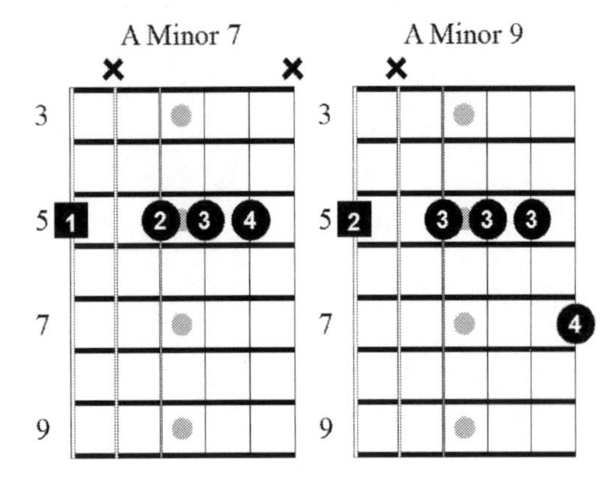

If you take a D7 chord and add the 2nd/9th note E, it becomes a D9.

Example 9j:

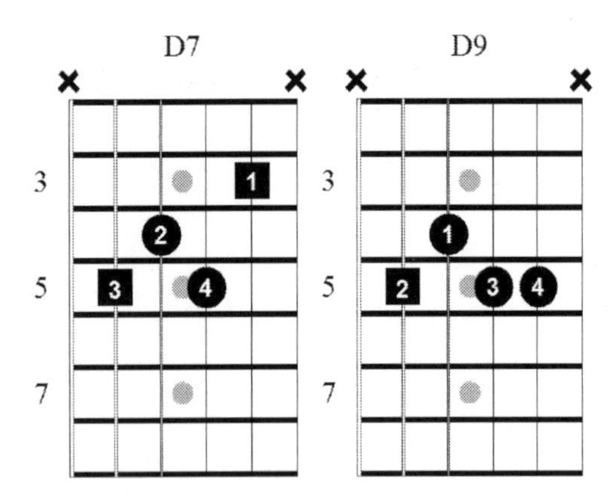

The same idea applies with 11ths and 13ths.

While this isn't an exhaustive discussion of every possible chord formed from the Major scale, it gives you enough grounding in the fundamentals to understand the second part of the book where we deal with modes, melody and soloing concepts.

If you want to get deep into chord construction and musical application, check out my book, **Guitar Chords in Context**.

How to Name Chords

Naming chords can be a bit subjective, although the system that is taught in most universities and music school revolves around whether the chord contains a 7th, and to a lesser extent, a third.

If a chord does **not** contain a 7th, then extensions are *generally* referred to by using the word 'add'.

For example, a C Major chord, (1 3 5) which has a 9th note added to it will be named Cadd9.

This name implies that there is no 7th.

By contrast, if we took a C Major 7th chord and added the 9th, the chord would be named C Major 9 or CMaj9:

Example 9k:

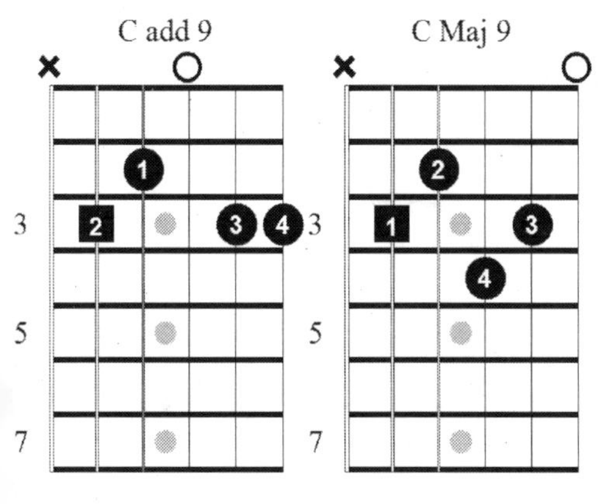

A G Major chord (1 3 5) with the 6th added is named G6 or 'G Major 6' whereas a G Major 7th chord (1 3 5 7) with the 6th (13th) added is named G Major 13:

Example 9l:

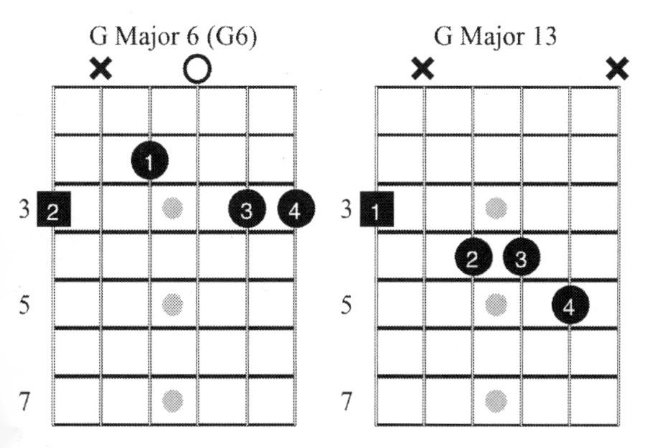

Similarly, a minor triad with the 9th added is named 'Minor add 9' and a Minor 7th chord with an added 9th is called Minor 9:

Example 9m:

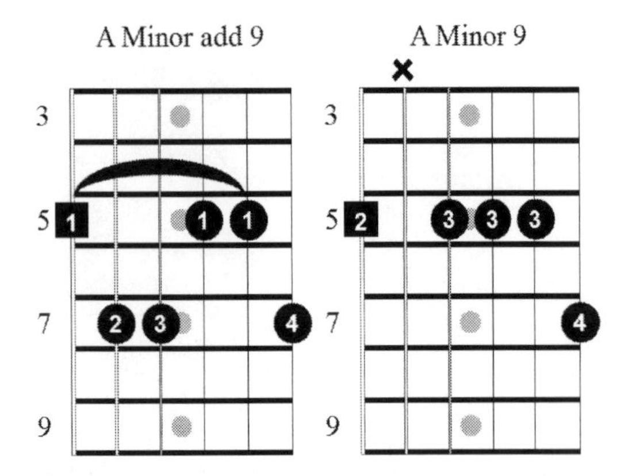

Dominant 7 chords *must* already contain the b7 note (1 3 5 b7) so extensions are simply named '9' '11' or '13', although often when we start adding higher extensions, some notes are omitted from the lower part of the chord to avoid undesirable clashes.

The most common note to be dropped is the 5th, but sometimes, especially in an '11' chord, the important 3rd may even be dropped. This dropping of the 3rd is more common on the guitar than other instruments due to fingering restraints. It is normally more desirable to drop the 5th or even the root than the 3rd.

Example 9n:

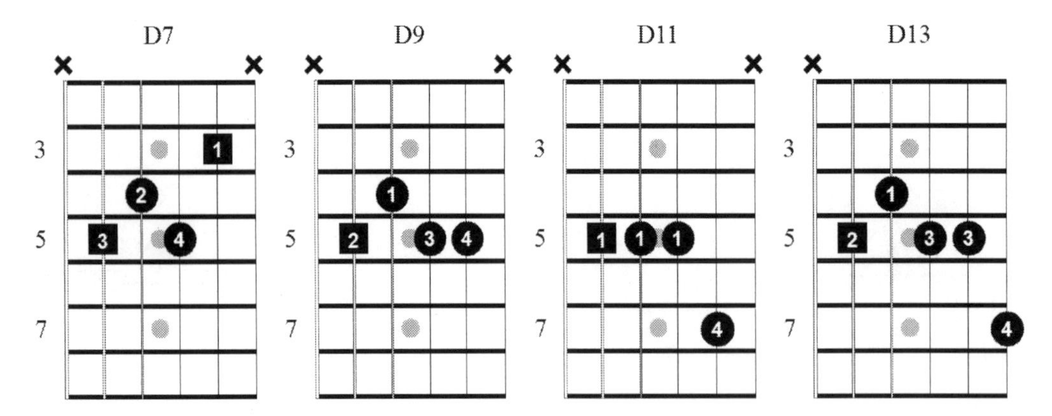

Remember the general rules:

If the 7th of a chord is included, then extensions are referred to as 9, 11 or 13.

If the 7th of a chord is not included, then extensions are referred to as 'add 9', 'add 11', or '6'.

Slight complications occur when the 3rd of a triad is *replaced* by a 2nd or 4th.

In D Major, the 3rd of the chord (F#) is played on the high E string:

D Major

If we *replace* the note F# with either the 2nd or 4th note from the scale, the D chord is said to be *suspended.* A suspended chord does not contain a 3rd. If we replace the F# with an E (2nd) we form the chord D Suspended 2nd or Dsus2, (1 2 5).

Example 9o:

D Sus 2

(The note E is played on the open 1st string). If we replace the F# with a G (4th) we form the chord D Suspended 4th or Dsus4, (1 4 5)

Example 9p:

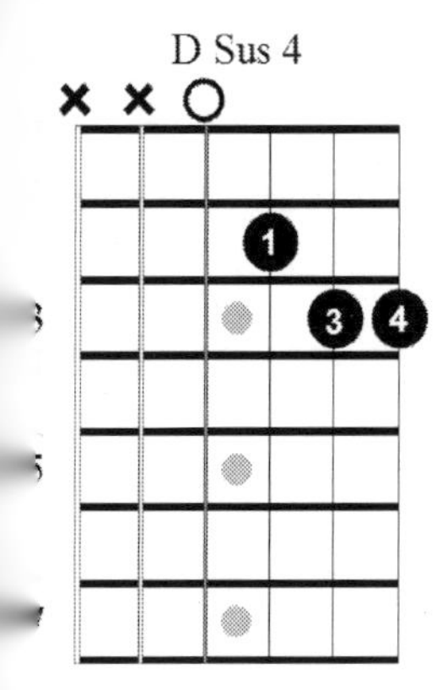

Because of the lack of a 3rd, these chords sound unresolved or 'suspended'

Part Two: Scales, Arpeggios, Modes, Soloing and Substitutions

The first part of this book a necessary grounding in the basics of chord theory. Part Two delves deeper into each of the *modes* of the Major scale. You will learn how to use arpeggios and pentatonic scales to create new, interesting sounds, and five useful modern licks for each mode to get you playing appropriate lead lines.

What is a Mode?

A mode is a scale which has been generated or *derived* from a *parent scale*. In this book we focus on the seven modes that can be derived from the Major scale.

To derive a mode from the Major scale, start on *any* note that isn't the root of the Major scale, and make that the root of a new scale. You then play through the notes of the parent scale *beginning and ending* on the new root.

For example, if we use the scale of C Major **C D E F G A B C** but begin on the note D, **D E F G A B C D**

We have created a new scale. In this case, we have created the *Dorian mode.* Even though the Dorian mode contains the same notes a C Major, because we start on a different rung of the ladder it has a different sequence of tones and semitones and therefore sounds completely different.

It is possible to begin on each note of the Major scale to create a new mode:

The notes E F G A B C D E is the *Phrygian mode.*

F to F is the *Lydian mode.*

G to G is the *Mixolydian mode.*

A to A is the *Aeolian mode.*

B to B is the *Locrian mode.*

Sometimes the parent Major scale, C to C is named the *Ionian* mode, however, that isn't common these days.

It's important to remember that most music for the past eight hundred years has been based around the Major scale and its harmony. Western ears have been conditioned since birth to hear melodies in relation to this Major scale.

Because the modes we use are *derived* from this Major scale and contain the same notes, playing them in isolation will tend to make you hear them as wanting to resolve to the root of the parent Major scale. This destroys the modal characteristics and the result is that you simply *hear* the Major scale starting from a different note. Playing through a mode without an appropriate backing track will generally cause your ears to want to resolve the mode back to the parent Major scale.

For example, play and listen to example 10a. It is one octave of the D Dorian mode. When you get to the bottom of the scale, do your ears want to continue on one more note to the C, the root of the parent scale?

Example 10a:

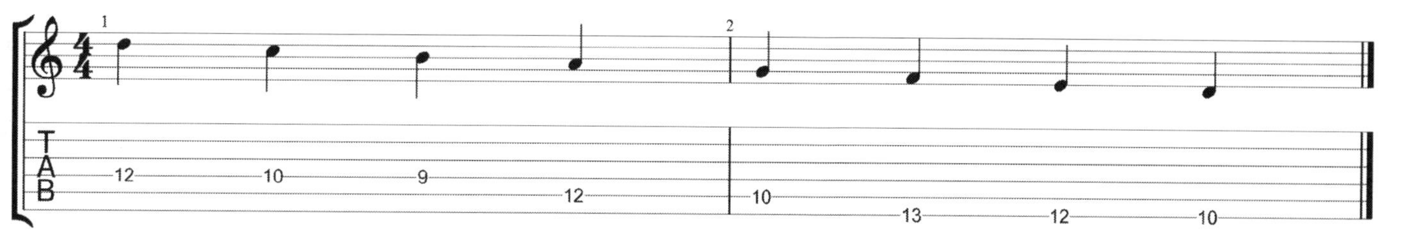

Now try listening to example 10b where I play the same thing but this time with a chordal backing track built from strong chords of the Dorian mode. Because your ears have *framed* the notes around these chords they will allow you to hear the notes in the context of the D root. In turn, all the scale steps (intervals) will be heard in relation to D, and the unique flavour of the Dorian mode will shine through.

Example 10b:

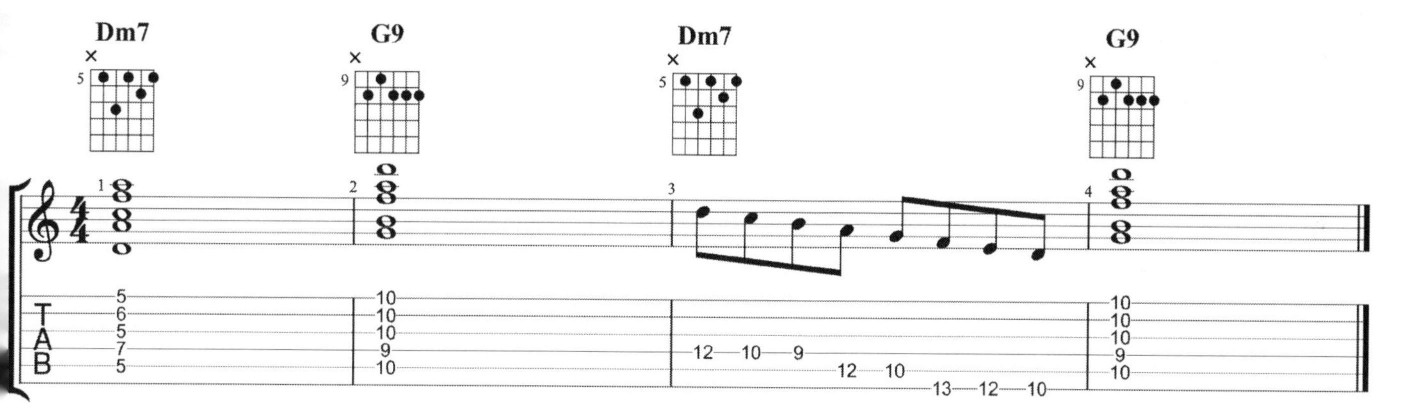

It is not always necessary to build a complex chord progression to hear its unique tonality. In rock music, power chords or simple riffs are used to outline a key centre with little more harmonic information than the root and 5th of each chord. In this book, however I will give you some specifically modal chord progressions which highlight the unique character of each mode.

Why do Modes Sound Different to the Major Scale?

Returning to the analogy of a scale being a ladder with rungs set in a specific pattern, a *mode* is simply a different spacing of these rungs. Because the rungs are spaced differently, the mode has a different sound. Also, the chord qualities on each harmonised scale note the chords different so the scale's harmony is different too.

For example, chord I in the Major scale is a Major 7th, but when we harmonise the Dorian mode, chord I is a Minor 7. Instantly we have created a different mood. By selecting chords carefully, it is possible to bring out the unique character of each modal sound.

Let's compare the scale pattern of the D Dorian mode to the D Major scale. The formula of the equivalent Major scale is always the reference for describing any musical sound.

The notes of D Dorian are **D E F G A B C D**

Example 10c:

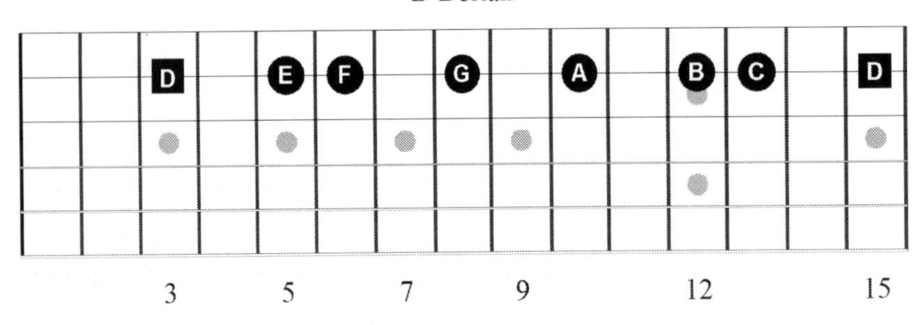

Whereas the notes of D Major are **D E F# G A B C# D**

Example 10d:

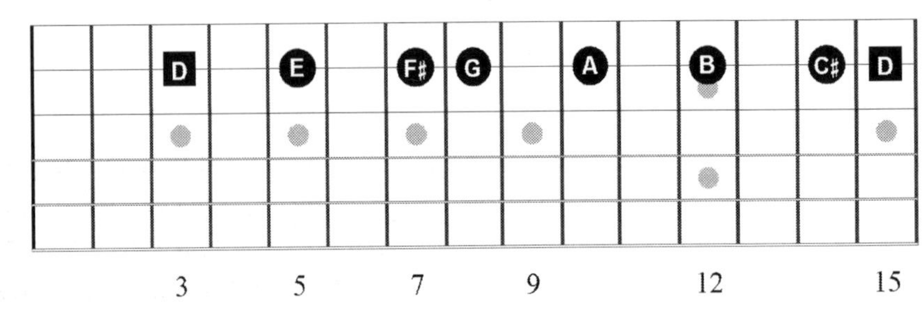

Instead of the F# in D Major, D Dorian contains an F Natural. In other words, the 3rd note, F# has been *flattened*. This is written as 'b3'.

Instead of the C# in D Major, D Dorian contains a C Natural. In other words, the 7th note, C# has been *flattened*. This is written as 'b7'.

Compared to the formula of the Major scale:**1 2 3 4 5 6 7**

The Dorian mode is described as :**1 2 b3 4 5 6 b7**

If you remember that minor *chords* always contain a b3, you will immediately realise that D Dorian will sound very different from D Major. The first chord, 1 b3 5 b7 outlines a Minor 7 chord so this mode is defined as a minor sound and will therefore have a sad-sounding feeling.

To recap:

The new pattern of tones and semitones in a mode creates a different mood from the original Major scale.

This mood is emphasised by playing the modal scale over chord progressions or riffs that outline chords derived from the harmonised mode.

It is important at first to learn a new modal scale over an appropriate chord progression that sets up the sound of the mode. The listener's ear must be taught that the mode does not resolve to the root of the parent Major scale. By framing the modal context of the scale with chords, the listener will accept and hear the new interval structure of the mode you are using.

Dissecting Modal Scales

Instead of soloing with scales as a long sequence of notes, the modern way to approach improvising is to split them up into smaller structures to create a more intervallic approach. Hiding within each scale are various melodic structures we can employ as unique soloing ideas. By viewing a scale as a set of smaller chunks, it is easy to find new ways to be creative. Instead of playing scalic ideas, we automatically introduce jumps and leaps into our playing which help to break up the monotony of long step-wise lines.

Another advantage is that we can cherry pick the colourful notes of a scale and imply its unique colour with only a limited number of notes.

Each scale can be broken down into the following structures:

2-Note Intervals

An interval is the distance between two notes. Just as we formed chords by leapfrogging one note in the Major scale, e.g. C – E, (intervals of a 3rd) we can jump other distances, for example C – F (4ths), C – G (5ths) etc. By skipping intervals, we start to break up the linear nature of a scale and introduce melodic leaps and patterns. While the overall tonality of the mode remains the same, you may be surprised at the different textures that can be created by 'thinking' in intervals instead of scales.

3-Note Triads

In Part One we used triads to form chords. A triad is three skipped 3rds, e.g. C – E – G. However, we don't have to play them as a chord. If we play the notes sequentially we generate many interesting melodic possibilities by leaving out most of the scale tones.

A triad, as you know, can be formed on every note of a scale, e.g. C-E-G, D-F-A, E-G-B etc. By picking out specific triads instead of playing full scales we can cherry pick the scale degrees that we include in our solos. With a triadic approach, instead of a scalic one, we not only isolate the specific tones we want to hear, we automatically introduce melodic leaps into our playing and avoid predictable scale runs. Triads do not have to be played in order, for example, C-E-G is the same triad as E-G-C.

4-Note Arpeggios

Similar to 3-note triads, 4-note arpeggios are triads that have an extra 3rd added on top (in other words, a 7th chord). Instead of playing the triad C-E-G, we extend it so it becomes an arpeggio C-E-G-B. Once again, we do not have to play these notes in order so the melodic permutations are massive. There is an arpeggio choice built off every note of each scale and again.

5-Note Pentatonic Scales

Most players see a chord progression in the key of A and immediately play an A Minor Pentatonic scale lick. However, you can build Minor Pentatonic scales on other degrees of any Major mode, not just the root.

There are *three* Minor Pentatonic scales hiding within each mode of the Major scale. Knowing where these are instantly allows us to use pentatonic licks we already know, but play them in different places in the scale to create a modal sound. As you can imagine, tripling your existing licks in this way is extremely useful.

In the following section I will teach you all the available structures in each mode, however, these possibilities can quickly become overwhelming when you are starting out. Most musicians, even accomplished ones, normally have a limited range of favourite approaches. To help get you started, I will give you my first-choice soloing structures at the end of each chapter. These are some useful practice ideas in the conclusion that will help you make music with the concepts in this section.

Dorian

The Dorian mode is very common in rock, funk, jazz and fusion music. It has a 'minor, but not too minor' characteristic that lends itself well to bluesy jazz solos. It is common to play Dorian over static (one chord) vamps of Minor 7, Minor 9 or Minor 11 chords.

Some important songs that use Dorian are:

- **So What** – Miles Davies
- **Billy Jean** – Michael Jackson
- **Tender Surrender** – Steve Vai (with a few key changes to related modes)

Formula and Harmonisation

As already seen, the formula of the Dorian mode is: **1 2 b3 4 5 6 b7**

And is played like this on the guitar. (The hollow dots are the *tonic* Minor 7 chord that you should visualise and hear when you play through the scale).

Example 11a:

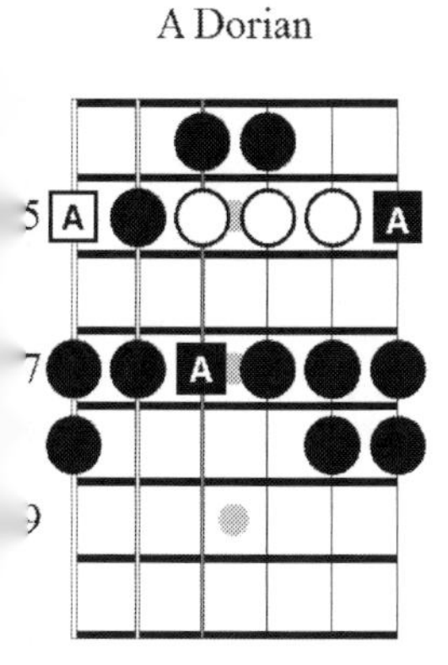

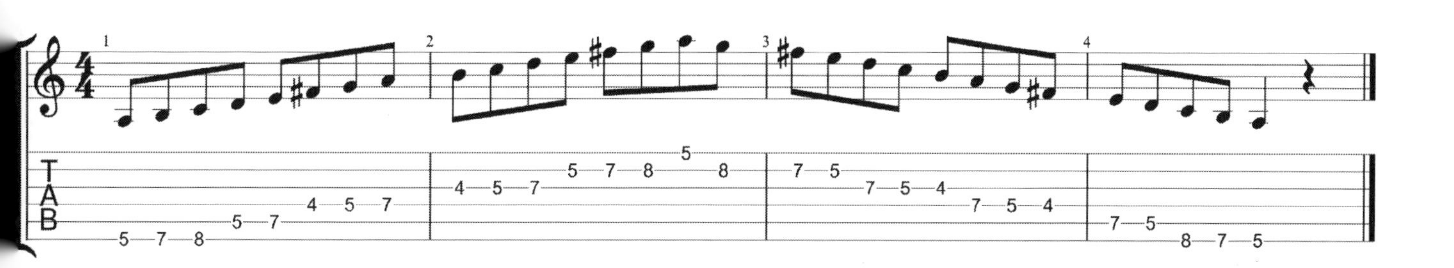

The Dorian mode generates the following set of chords:

TRIAD Chord Type	SEVENTH Chord Types	Example in the key of A Dorian
I Minor	i Minor 7 (extensions 9, 11, 13)	A Minor 7
ii Minor	ii Minor 7 (extensions b9, 11, b13)	B Minor 7
III Major	III Major 7 (extensions 9, #11, 13)	C Major 7
IV Major	IV 7 (extensions 9, 11, 13)	D7
V Minor	v Minor7 (extensions 9, 11, b13)	E Minor 7
vi Minor b5	vi Minor 7b5 (extensions b9, 11, b13)	F#m7b5
VII Major	VII Major 7 (extensions 9, 11, 13)	G Major 7

You will often see extended chords such as 9ths, 11ths and 13ths used in a progression. By adding upper extensions, a modal sound can be defined more accurately.

For example, Dorian is the only mode to have a b3, natural 11 and natural 13. By playing a Minor 13 chord with the 11th included you completely define the Dorian sound. However, this harmonic density is normally too high to be palatable to the listener. Often, Minor 7 chords will be played with a just one extension, and other scale extensions are contained in other chords in the progression. For example, the note G is the 11th note of the Dorian scale, but it can be played in an E minor chord (E-G-B)

Typical Dorian Chord Progressions

The following chord progressions outline the unique character of the Dorian mode. For simplicity, they are all in the key of A, but you should transpose them into different keys using the techniques in Part One.

Example 11b:

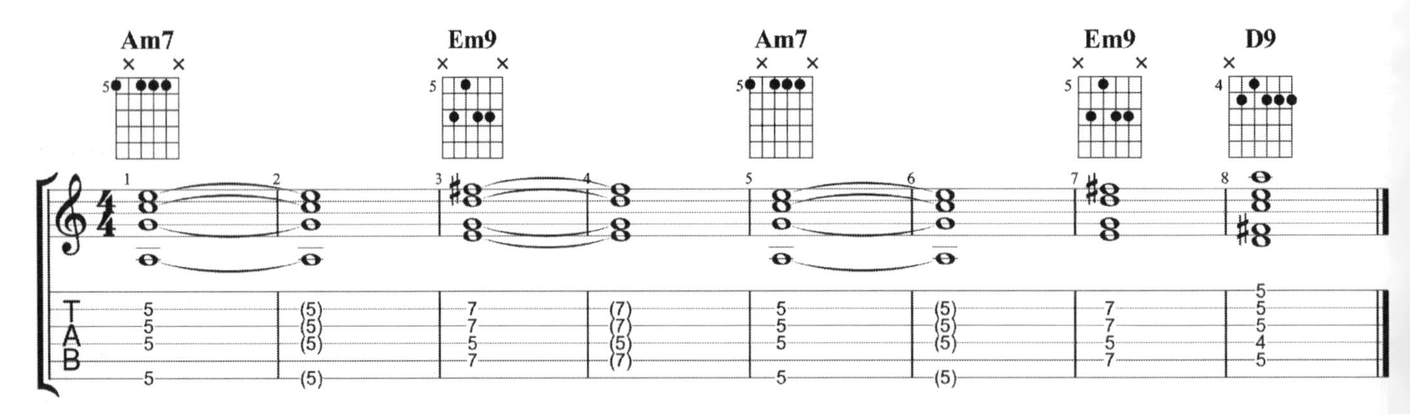

Example 11c:

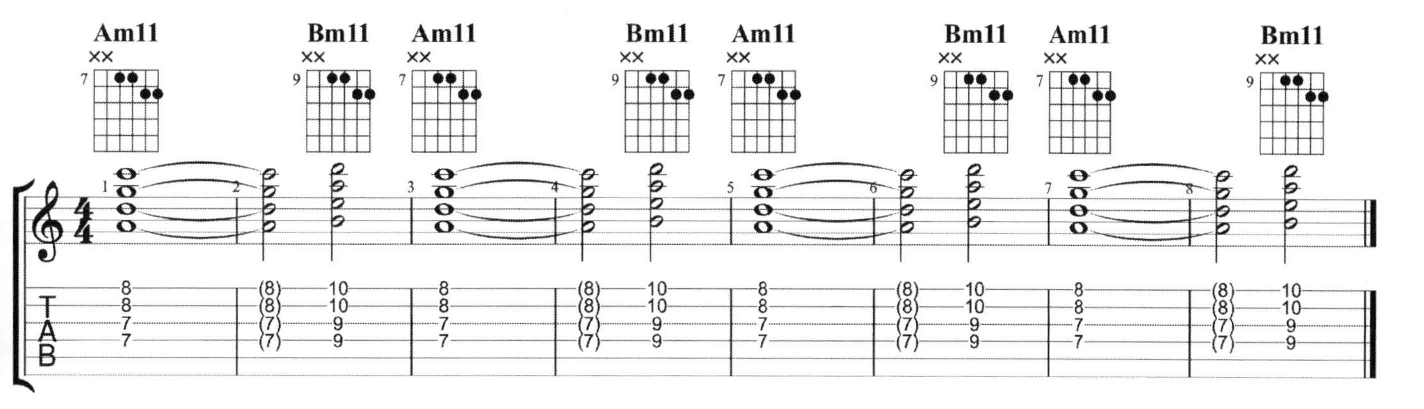

Example 11d:

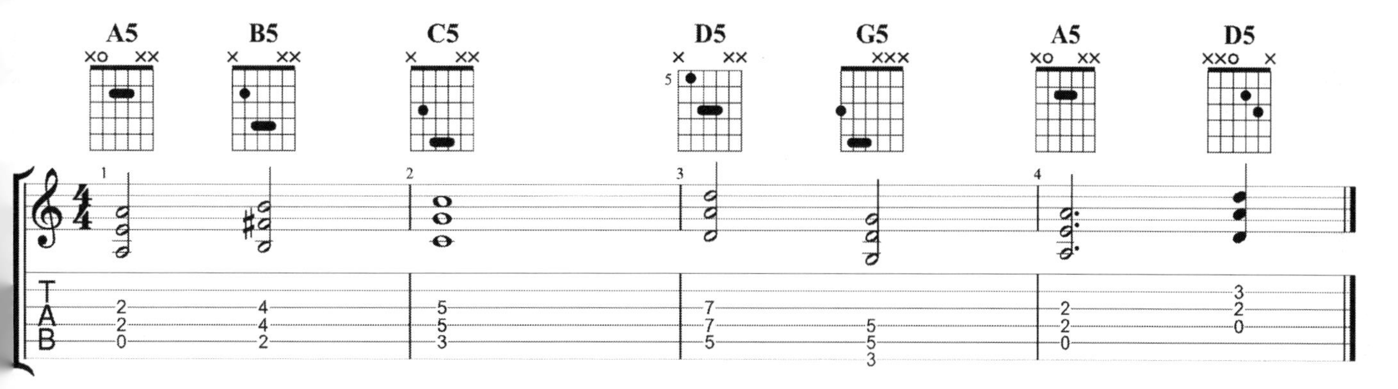

5 Useful Dorian Licks

The following five licks use the Dorian mode in its first position. They are all included as audio examples and the Dorian backing track has kindly been provided by **Quist**.

Example 11e:

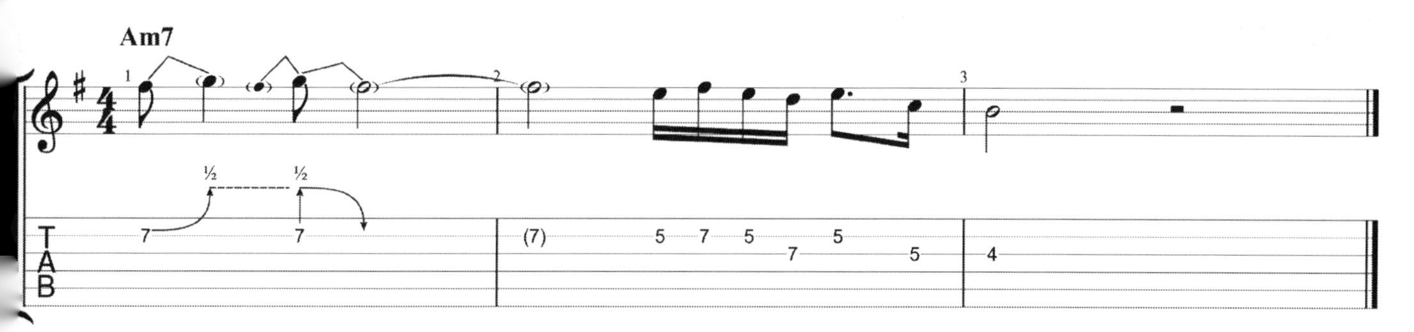

Example 11f:

Example 11g:

Example 11h:

Example 11i:

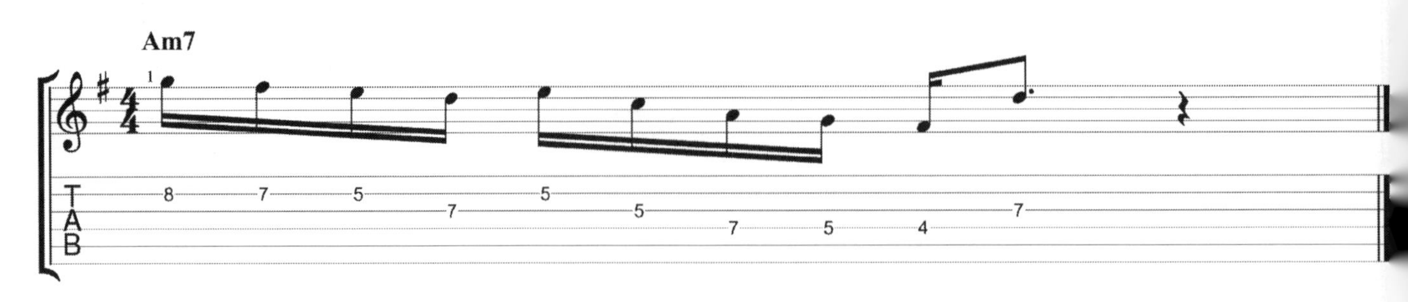

Soloing Approaches to the Dorian Mode

The following pages analyse the ways we can dissect the Dorian Mode. Each approach (intervals, triads, arpeggios and pentatonic scales) is one 'level' of depth we can explore to create melodic ideas. Think of each structure as an increasingly dense layer of melodic complexity. All the structures can be freely combined to make a solo. Try each idea over the Dorian backing track to get a feel for the texture of each melodic concept.

2-Note Intervals

Example 12a: A Dorian in 3rds:

Example 12b: A Dorian in 4ths:

Example 12c: A Dorian in 5ths:

Example 12d: A Dorian in 6ths:

Example 12e: A Dorian in 7ths:

Try reversing certain interval patterns, for example, play one 3rd ascending and one 3rd descending:

Example 12f:

Or ascending two 3rds and descending one third:

Example 12g:

This kind of 'permutation' approach can be of real benefit when you want to create new licks or lines and can be applied to any of the above interval distances.

I'm a big fan of using 4ths and 6ths in Dorian.

3-Note Triads

Triads (stacked 3rds) can be constructed from each of the degrees of the A Dorian mode. By combining just one or two triads built from a mode, we can target specific intervals or 'colour tones'. If we play a B Minor triad over an A Dorian chord sequence, you exclusively targeting the extensions 9, 11, and 13 (B, D and F#). This sounds very different from playing an E Minor triad over the same backing, as the E Minor triad would target the 5th, b7 and 9th degrees of the scale.

Triads from each degree are shown here, first in one octave (12h), and then in two octaves (12i).

Example 12h:

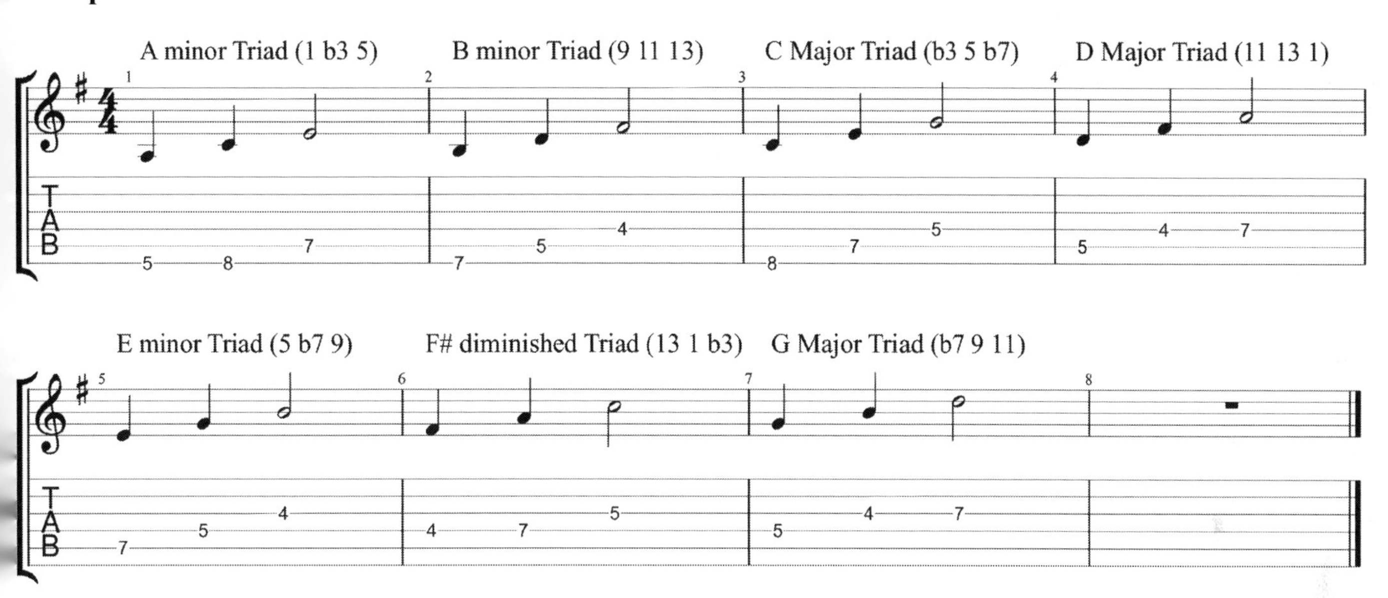

Example 12i:

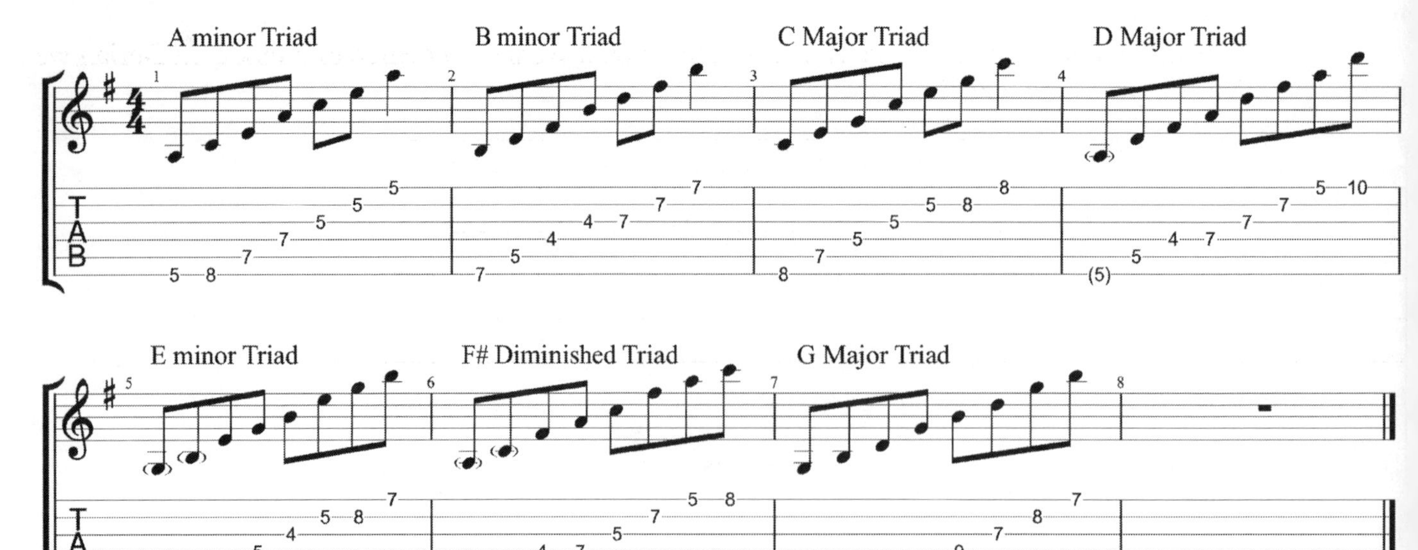

You will soon learn which type of triad is formed from each degree of each mode. For reference, here is the list of triads built from each degree of the Dorian mode:

Scale Degree	3-Note Triads Built in Dorian	Intervals Against Tonic
1	I Minor	1, b3, 5
2	ii Minor	9, 11, 13
b3	bIII Major	b3, 5, b7
4	IV Major	11, 13, 1
5	v Minor	5, b7, 9
6	vi Minor b5	13, 1, b3
b7	bVII Major	b7, 9, 11

At first it may seem overly complex to think, "OK, I can play a Minor triad off the 5th degree of Dorian..." so instead learn these triad approaches as simple shapes or patterns contained within the parent mode. Once you have improvised with each one in turn, pick your one or two favourite sounds and stick to them. Don't worry about the ones you're not learning, focus only on making new patterns and inversions out of a limited range of triadic material.

The triads I like to use in Dorian are:

Minor b5 off the 6th degree (F# Minor b5 triad over A Dorian) (13, 1 and b3)

Major off the b7 (G Major over A Dorian) (b7 9 and 11)

4-Note Arpeggios

Arpeggios (three stacked 3rds) for example, A-C-E-G can be built from each degree of a mode. In Dorian we generate the following 4-note arpeggios:

Scale Degree	4-Note Arpeggios in Dorian	Intervals Against Tonic
1	i Minor 7	1, b3, 5, b7
2	ii Minor 7	9, 11, 13, 1
b3	bIII Major 7	b3, 5, b7, 9
4	IV 7	11, 13, 1, b3
5	v Minor7	5, b7, 9, 11
6	vi Minor 7b5	13, 1, b3, 5
b7	bVII Major 7	b7, 9, 11, 13

As they contain an additional note to triads, they create a more dense quality in your solos.

Arpeggios from each degree of A Dorian can be played in the following manner:

Example 12j:

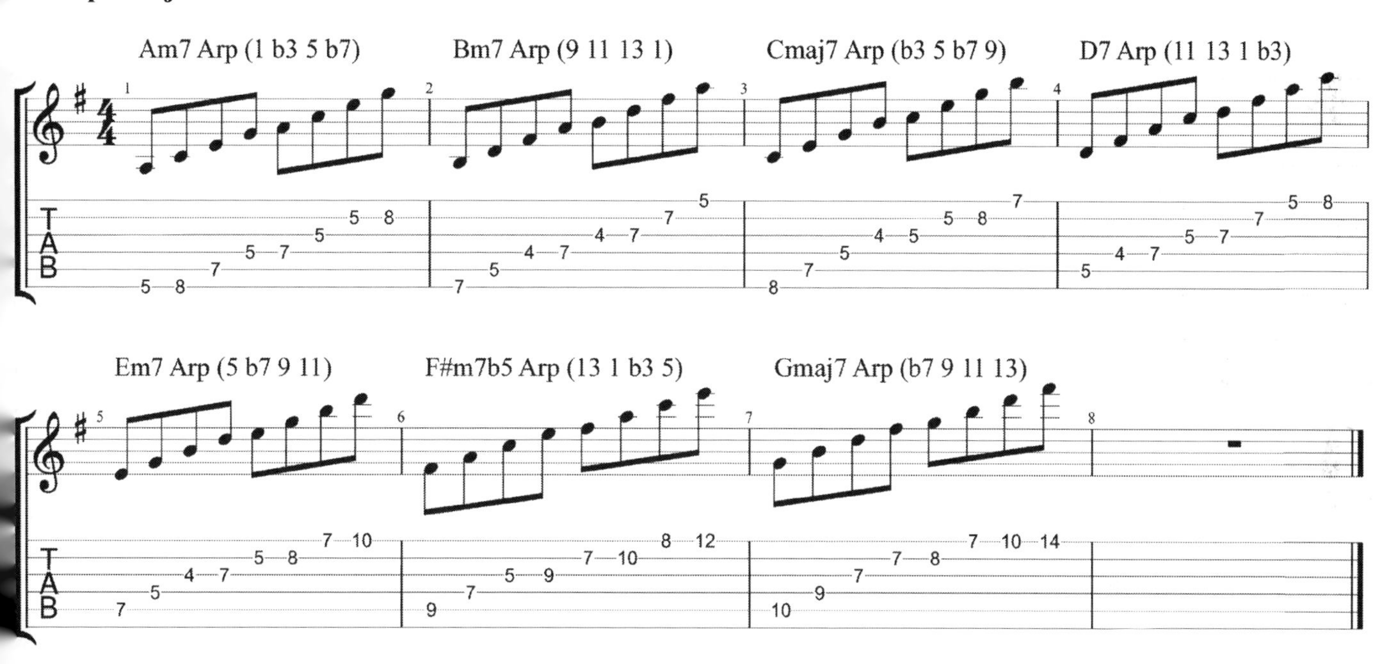

Play through these arpeggio ideas one-at-a-time over a backing track. Write down any that you like the sound of and focus on only those arpeggios. Play the arpeggio notes in different orders and in different sequences. Instead of 1357, try 1537 or 17135. The possibilities are endless.

My favourite approaches are to play these arpeggios:

Major 7th on the b3 (C Major 7 over A Dorian) (b3 5 b7 9).

Major 7th off the b7 (G Major 7 over A Dorian) (b7 9 11 13).

5-Note Pentatonic Scales

One important, but often overlooked soloing concept is to superimpose Minor Pentatonic scales that you already know to highlight certain modal colour tones. Hiding inside each mode of the Major scale are three different 'standard' Minor Pentatonic scales.

The diagram below shows the scale of A Dorian with the scale of A Minor Pentatonic running through it. The hollow dots show the Minor Pentatonic scale, and the solid dots are the Dorian mode. By playing an A Minor Pentatonic scale over an A Dorian chord progression, we highlight the scale tones **1 b3 11 5 b7**. This, as you might imagine, sounds quite conventional and 'bluesy'.

Example 12k: A Minor Pentatonic over A Dorian:

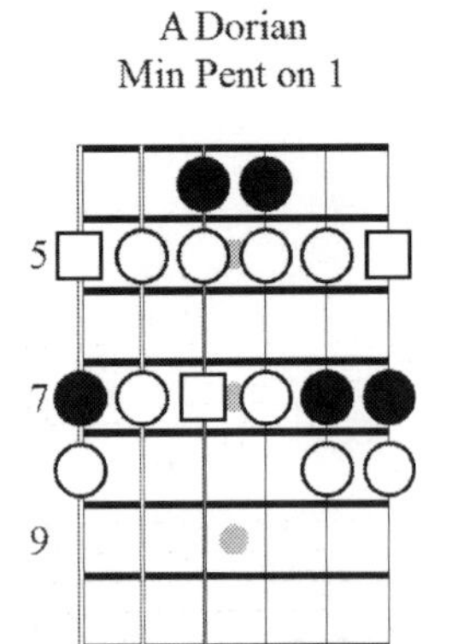

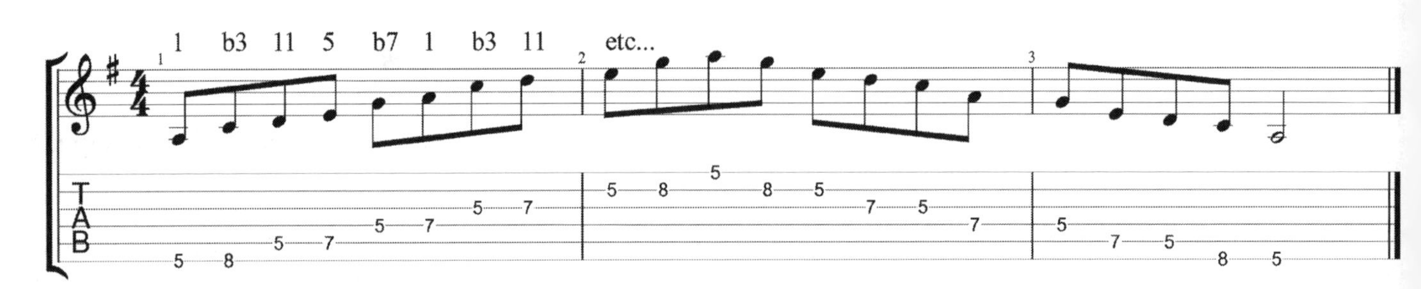

While this is a fairly obvious approach, you may not realise that there are two more Minor Pentatonic scales contained within the parent mode. You can also play a Minor Pentatonic scale from the 5th (E).

Example 12l: Minor Pentatonic on the 5th:

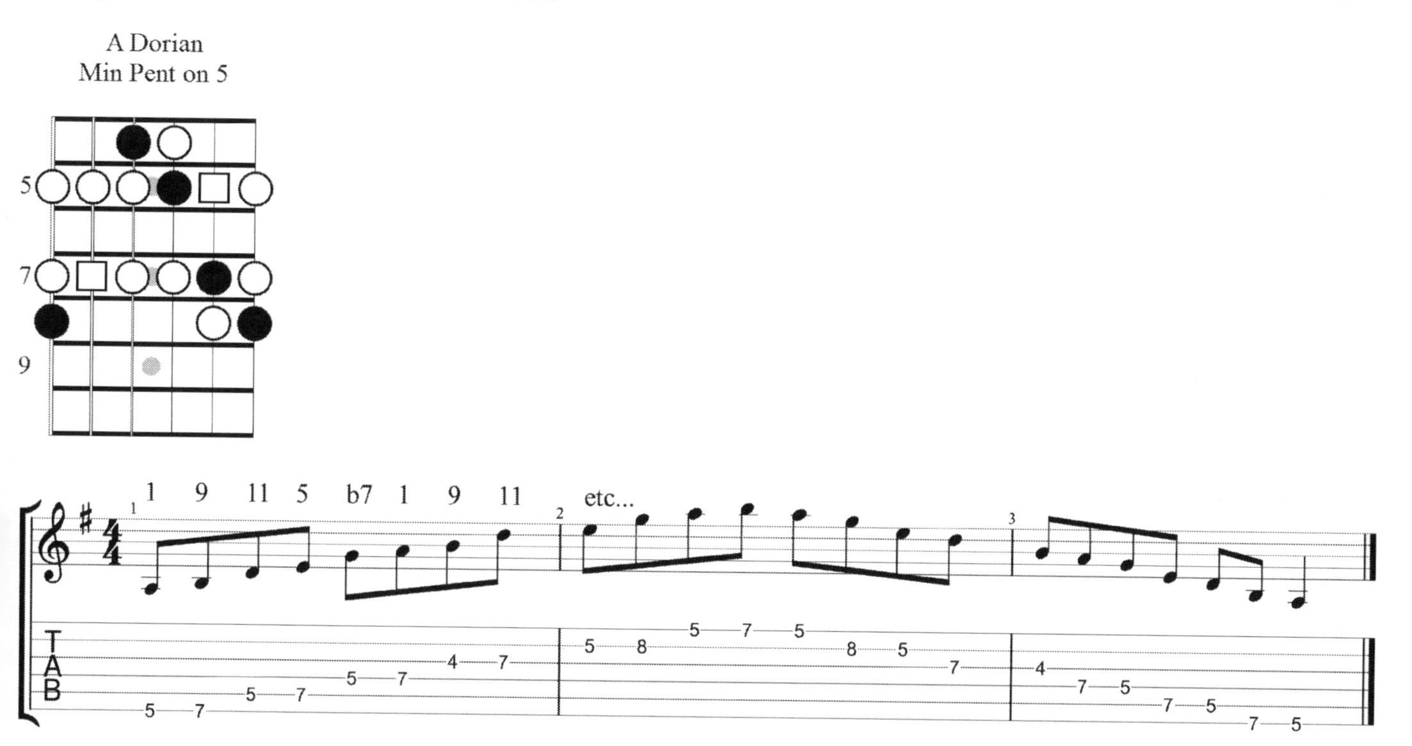

When you play E Minor Pentatonic over A Dorian, you target the Dorian intervals **1, 9, 11, 5, b7**. This is a great sound and my favourite Dorian soloing approach.

You can also play a Minor Pentatonic scale on the 9th *(or 2nd)* degree of the Dorian mode. This is a little harder to handle over an A Dorian groove when played in isolation, but don't forget you can also play A Minor Pentatonic over A Dorian too! You now have access to both A Minor, and B Minor Pentatonic scales. This means that any A Minor idea you play can be shifted up a tone and repeated to form Dorian sequences. This is an excellent approach and really helps to build longer melodic lines.

Example 12m: Minor Pentatonic on the 9th (2nd)

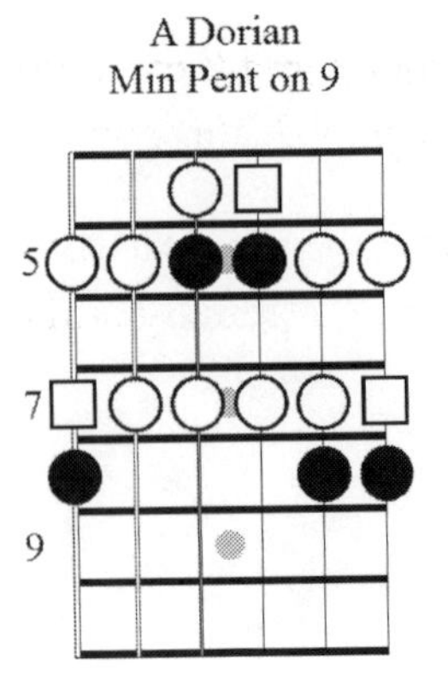

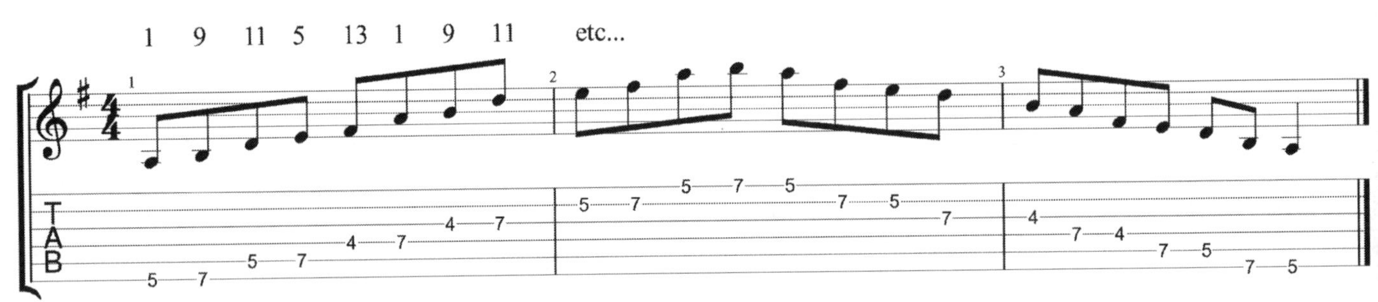

In summary, when you are using the Dorian mode, you can play Minor Pentatonic scales on the root, 9th (2nd) and 5th. My favourite in isolation is to play Minor Pentatonic on the 5th of Dorian.

First Choice Soloing Summary for the Dorian Mode

Parent Scale: Dorian

Intervals: 4ths and 6ths

Triads: Minor b5 from the 6th degree / Major from b7

Arpeggio: Major 7th on the b3 / Major 7th off the b7

Pentatonic: Minor Pentatonic on the 5th

Phrygian

The Phrygian mode isn't commonly used in pop, but it isn't unusual to find it in heavy rock, metal and flamenco. It has a uniquely dark yet palatable sound with the unusual b9 degree giving it a somewhat Spanish flavour.

Phrygian is often used to solo over power chords in rock music, but is rarely used to create diatonic chord progressions. As Phrygian is similar in construction to the Aeolian mode, they are often used interchangeably with one another.

Compositions that make use of the Phrygian mode:

- **War** – Joe Satriani
- **Wherever I May Roam** – Metallica

Formula and Harmonisation

The formula for the Phrygian mode is **1 b2 b3 4 5 b6 b7**

It is played like this on the guitar in the key of A:

Example 13a:

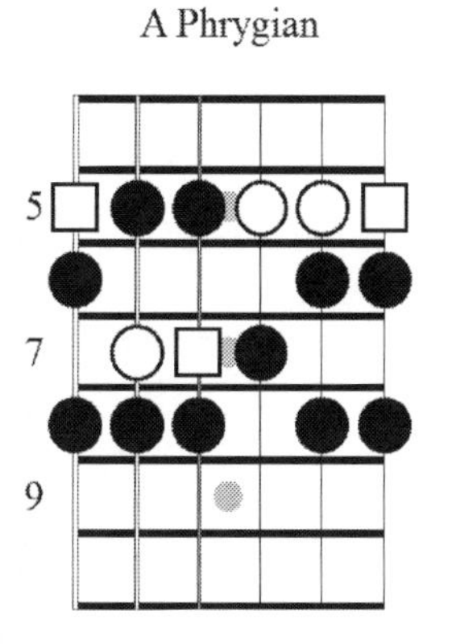

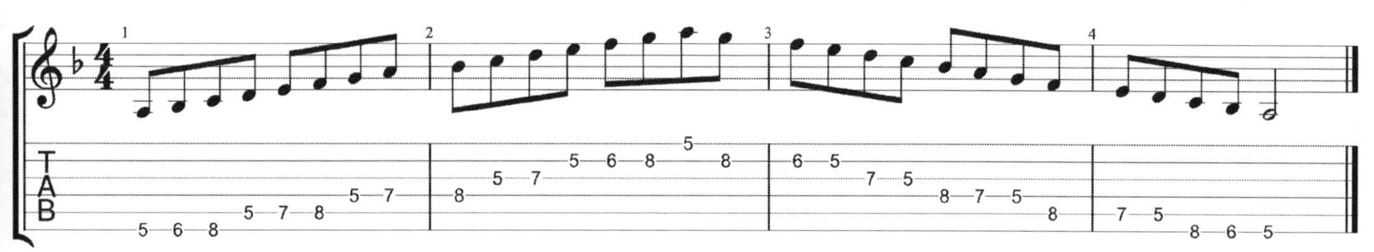

Visualise the Phrygian mode around the A Minor chord highlighted.

When harmonised, Phrygian gives the following series of chords:

TRIAD Chord Type	SEVENTH Chord Types	Example in the key of A Phrygian
i Minor	i Minor 7 (extensions b9, 11, b13)	A Minor 7
bII Major	bII Major 7 (extensions 9, #11, 13)	Bb Major 7
biii Major	biii 7 (extensions 9, 11, 13)	C7
iv Minor	iv Minor 7 (extensions 9, 11, b13)	D Minor 7
v Minor b5	V Minor 7b5 (extensions b9, 11, b13)	E Minor 7b5
bVI Major	bVI Major 7 (extensions 9, 11, 13)	F Major 7
bvii Minor	bvii Minor 7 (extensions 9, 11, 13)	G Minor 7

Due to Phrygian's dark nature, chord progressions using only diatonic chords can sound somewhat awkward. In rock music we can get around this by using riff-based power chord backings and soloing over them with the Phrygian mode. We can also use *upper structure triads* (slash chords) to imply the complex Phrygian harmony over a simple bass pattern.

Typical Phrygian Chord Progressions

Example 13b:

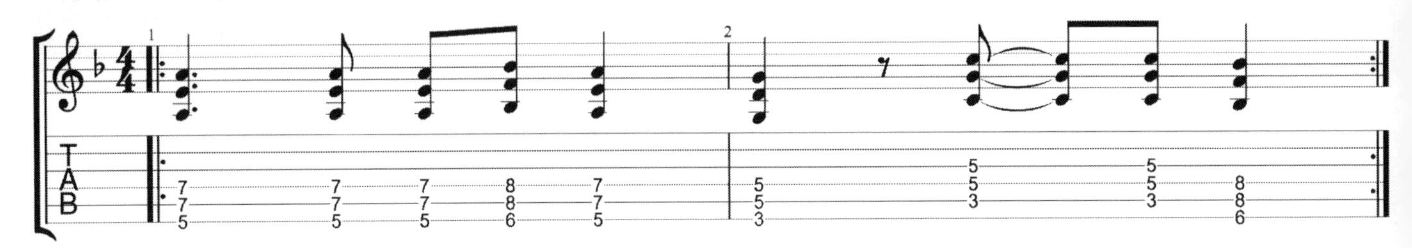

Example 13c:

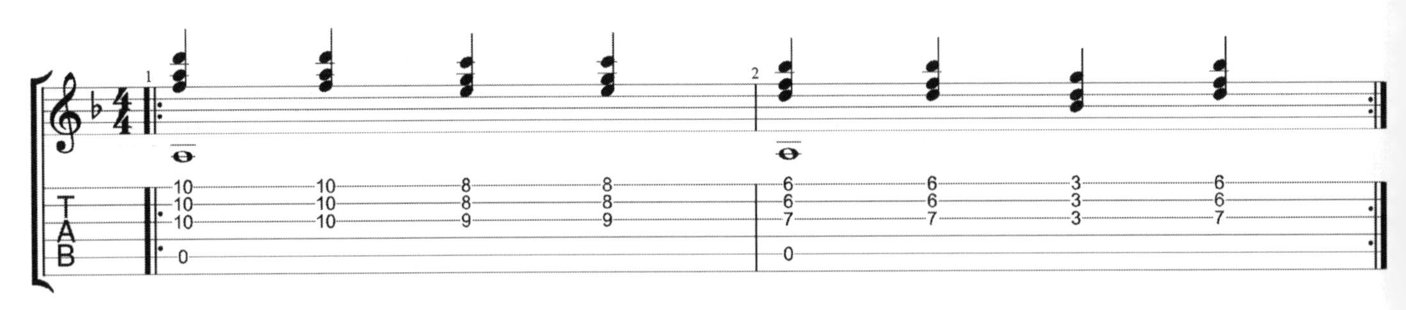

5 Useful Phrygian Licks

These licks are all included as audio examples and the Phrygian backing track has kindly been provided by **Quist**.

Example 13d:

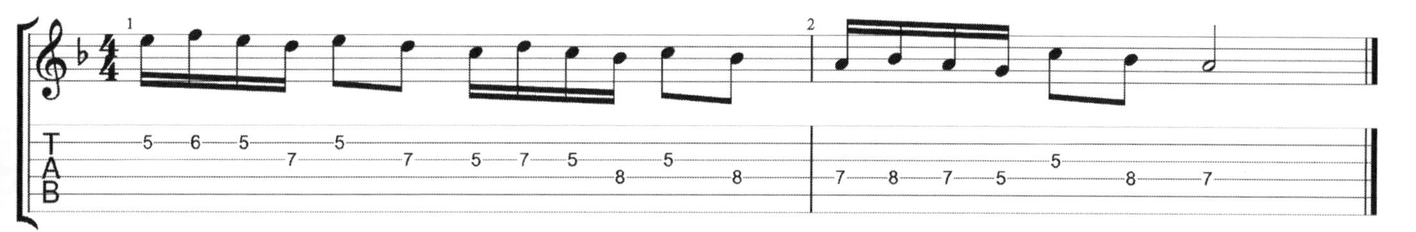

Example 13e:

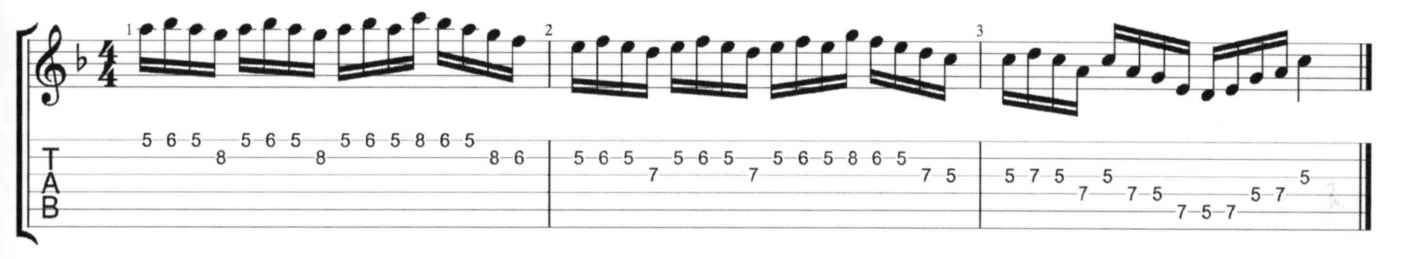

Example 13f:

Example 13g:

Example 13h:

Soloing Approaches to the Phrygian Mode

The following pages analyse the approaches we can take to dissect the A Phrygian Mode. Each approach (intervals, triads etc.), represents one level of density we can investigate to create melodic ideas. Think of each level as different layers of increasing complexity. Every structure can be freely combined to make a solo. Try each idea over the Phrygian backing track to get a feel for the texture of each melodic concept.

2-Note Intervals

Example 13h1:

Example 13i:

Example 13j:

Example 13k:

Example 13l:

My first interval choice in Phrygian is usually **3rds and 6ths**, but as always spend time practicing the ideas that you enjoy the most.

3-Note Triads

By isolating triads built from each degree of the Phrygian mode, we can be specific about the intervals of the mode that we target when soloing. The triads from each scale degree are shown below and the intervals formed against the root note (A) are given.

Example 13m:

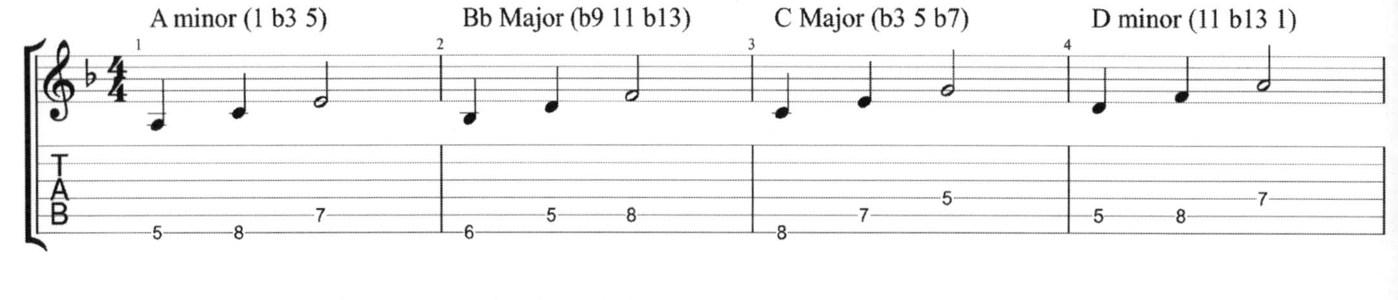

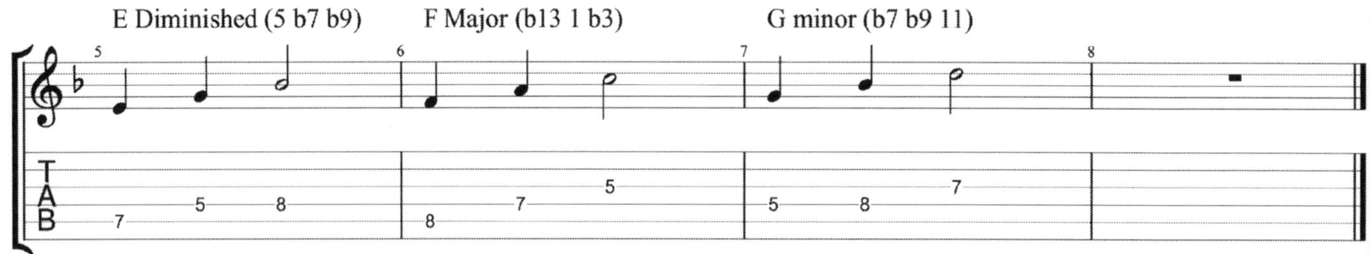

Example 13n:

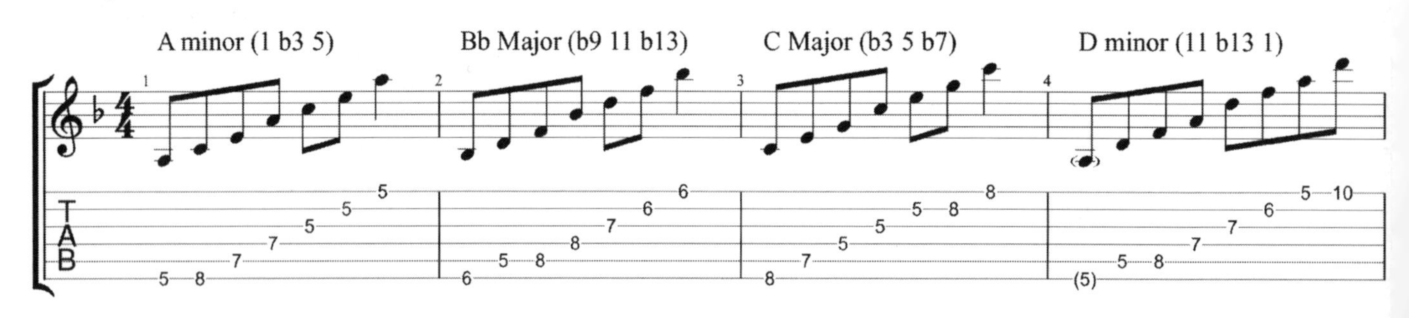

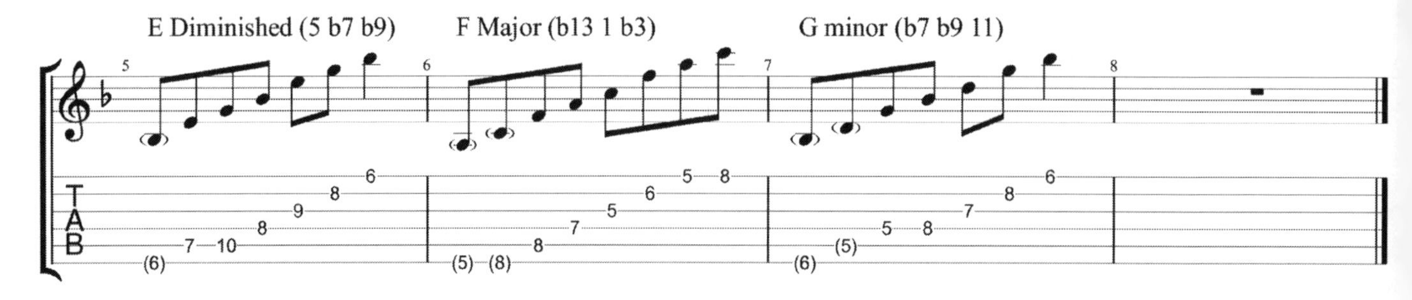

For reference, here is the list of triad chord types for Phrygian and the intervals they impose against the tonic:

Scale Degree	3-Note Triads Built in Phrygian	Intervals Against Tonic
1	i Minor	1, b3, 5
b2	bII Major	b9, 11, b13
b3	biii Major	b3, 5, b7
4	iv Minor	11, b13, 1
5	v Minor b5	5, b7, b9
b6	bVI Major	b13, 1, b3
b7	bvii Minor	b7, b9, 11

As a starting point for your studies, my favourite triads to solo with are:

Minor on the b7 (G Minor over A Phrygian) (b7, b9 b3).

Major on the b2 (Bb Major over A Phrygian) (b9, 11, b13).

Try making melodies using just one, or a combination of both these triads.

4-Note Arpeggios

Adding another 3rd interval to a triad creates a 4-note arpeggio. By building arpeggios on each degree of the Phrygian mode and soloing *only* using these arpeggios, we can be selective about which intervals of the scale we play. The arpeggios and intervals formed from the root of the Phrygian mode are shown in this table:

Scale Degree	4-Note Arpeggios in Phrygian	Intervals Against Tonic
1	i Minor 7	1, b3, 5, b7
b2	bII Major 7	b9, 11, b13, 1
b3	biii 7	b3, 5, b7, b9
4	iv Minor 7	11, b13, 1, b3
5	v Minor 7b5	5, b7, b9, 11
b6	bVI Major 7	b13, 1, b3, 5
b7	bvii Minor 7	b7, b9, 11, b13

Some will sound better than others to your ears, so put on the Phrygian backing track and experiment by jamming with one of the following arpeggios each time. Here they are shown in two octaves:

Example 13o:

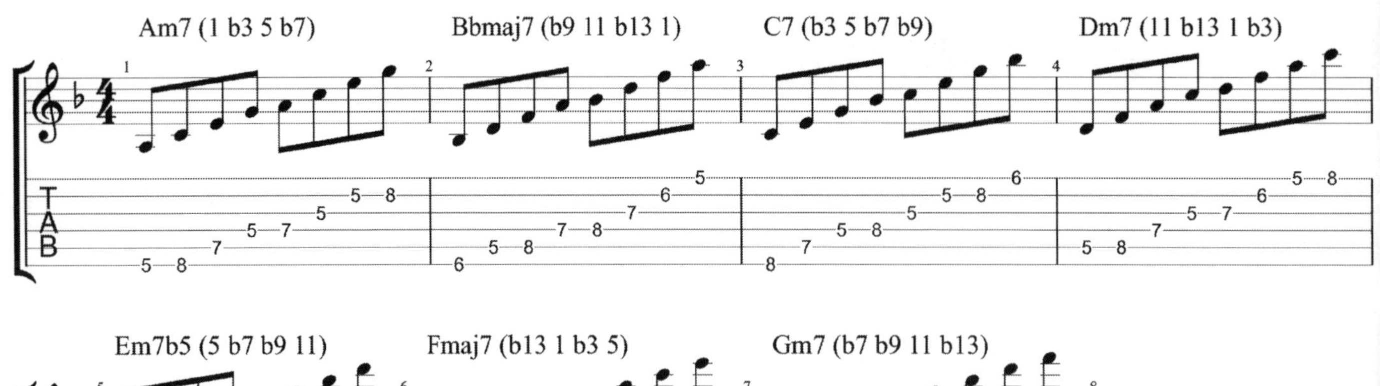

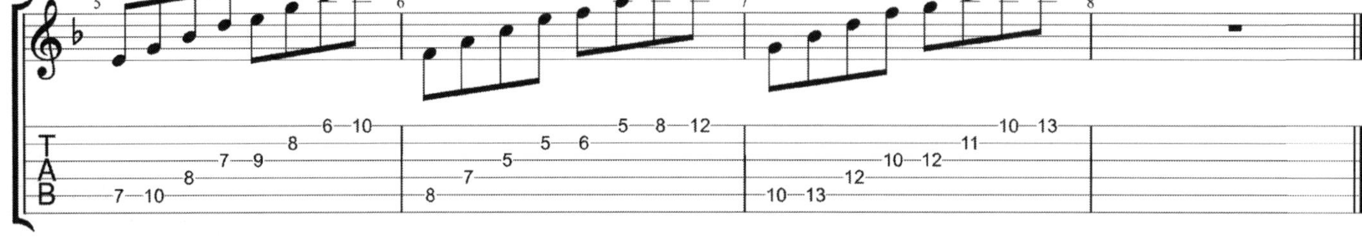

My first choices are to play:

Dominant 7 Arpeggio on the b3 (C7 over A) (b3 5 b7 b9).

Minor 7 Arpeggio on the b7 (G Minor 7 over A) (b7 b9 11 b13).

5-Note Pentatonic Scales

The three Minor Pentatonic scales in the Phrygian mode are on the root, the b7 and the 11(4). The following examples show how the pentatonic scales ‘fit’ inside the Phrygian shape:

Example 13p: Minor Pentatonic on the root:

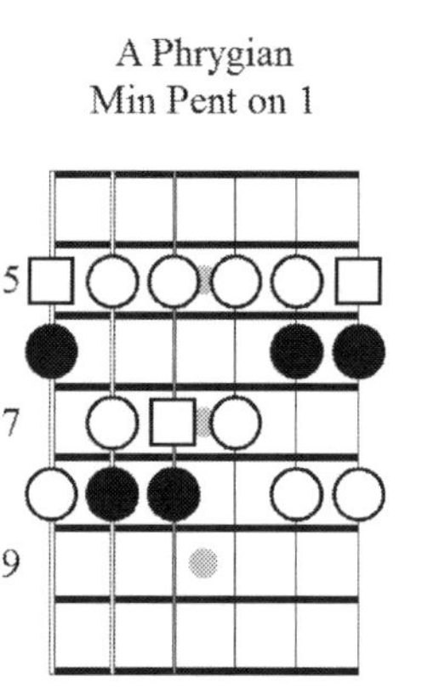

Minor Pentatonic from the root (A minor Pentatonic over A)

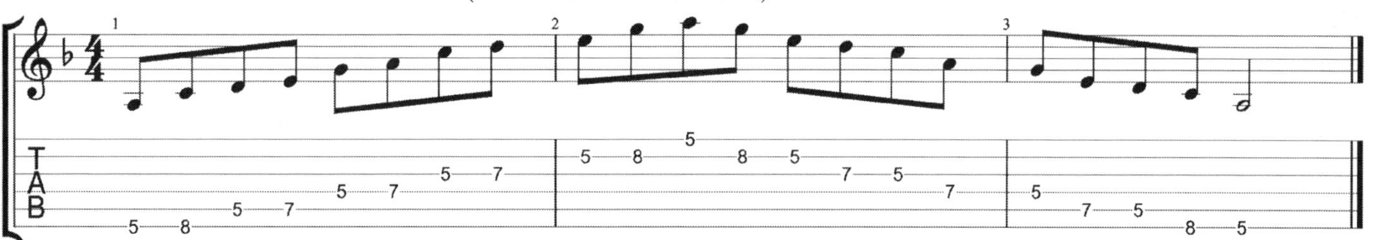

Intervals played against the root of Phrygian: **1, b3, 11, 5, b7**.

Example 13q: Minor Pentatonic on the b7:

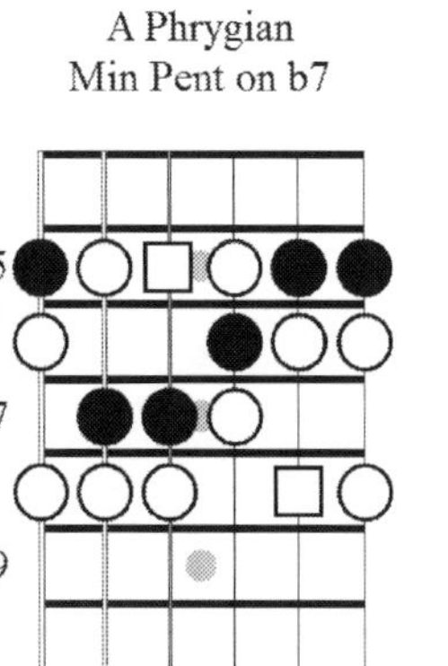

Minor Pentatonic from the b7 (G minor Pentatonic over A)

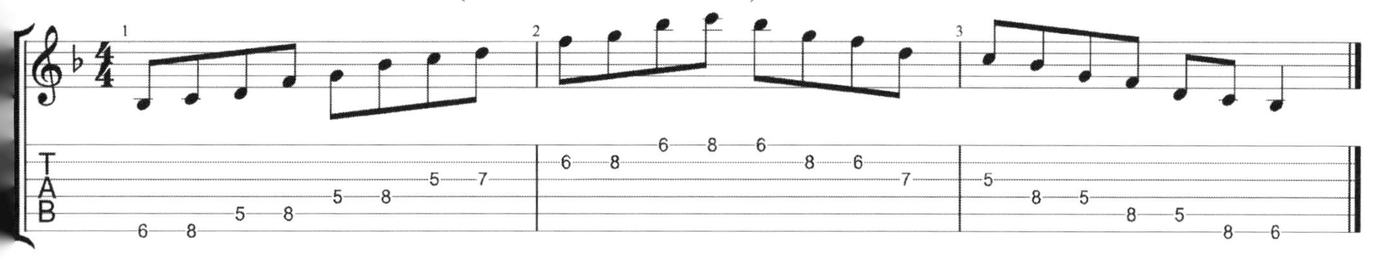

Intervals played against the root: **b3, 11, 5, b7, b9**.

Example 13r: Minor Pentatonic on the 11:

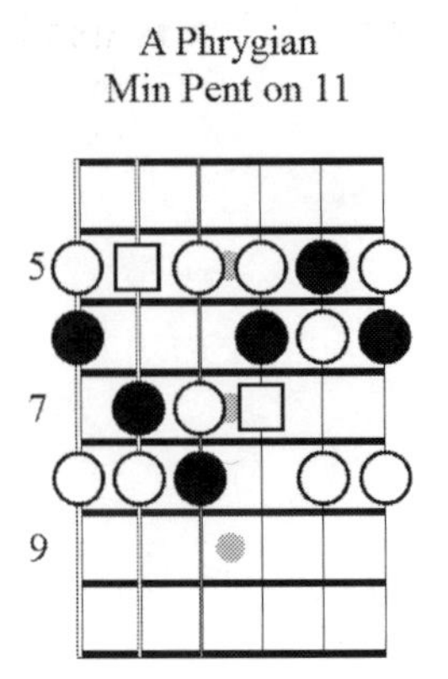

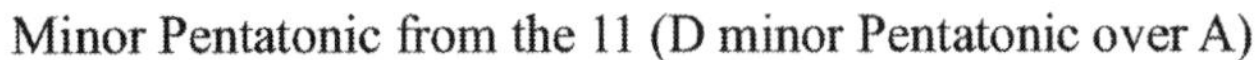

Intervals played against the root: **1, b3, 11, b13, b7**. I often use Minor Pentatonic scales played from the b7 and 11

First Choice Soloing Summary for the Phrygian Mode

Parent Scale: Phrygian.

Intervals: 3rds and 6ths.

Triads: Minor on the b7 / Major on the b2.

Arpeggio: Major 7th on the b3 / Major 7th on the b7.

Pentatonic: Minor Pentatonic on the b7 and 11.

Lydian

In my opinion, Lydian is one of the most beautiful, emotive tonalities in music. It contains just one note that is different from the Major scale, but this small alteration completely changes its character. Lydian is used extensively in rock guitar ballads by players like Steve Vai and Joe Satriani.

Songs constructed around the Lydian mode:

- **Flying in a Blue Dream** – Joe Satriani
- **How I Miss You** – Foo Fighters
- The introduction to **Hole Hearted** – Extreme
- **Answers** – Steve Vai
- **Shut up 'n Play Yer Guitar** – Frank Zappa

Formula and Harmonisation

The formula for the Lydian mode is **1 2 3 #4 5 6 7** (Only one note different from the Major scale). The #4 is normally referred to as a #11.

Example 14a:

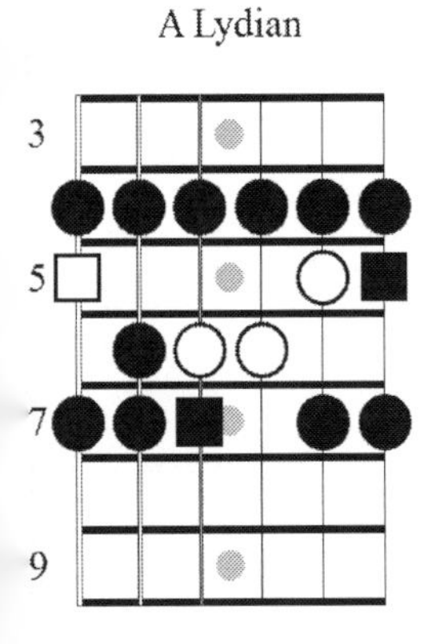

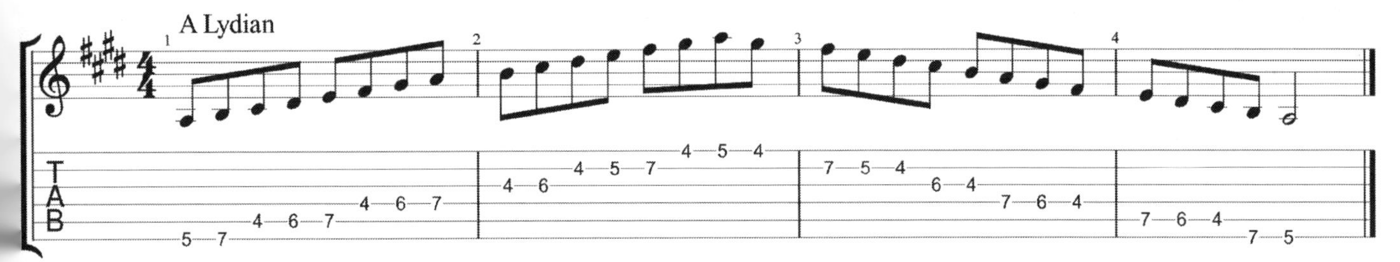

Learn to see and hear all the notes in this mode around the highlighted A Major 7th chord.

When harmonised, Lydian creates the following sequence of chords:

TRIAD Chord Type	SEVENTH Chord Types	Example in the key of A Lydian
I Major	I Major 7 (extensions 9, #11, 13)	A Major 7 (#11)
II Major	II7 (extensions 9, 11, 13)	B7
iii Minor	iii Minor 7 (extensions 9, 11, b13)	C# Minor 7
#iv Minor b5	#iv Minor 7b5 (extensions b9, 11, b13)	D# Minor 7b5
V Major	V Major 7 (extensions 9, 11, 13)	E Major 7
vi Minor	vi Minor 7 (extensions 9, 11, 13)	F# Minor 7
vii Minor	vii Minor 7 (extensions b9, 11, b13)	G# Minor 7

Typical Lydian Chord Progressions

When writing chord progressions that highlight the characteristics of Lydian, varying techniques are used. Often in it is played over a static vamp, and sometimes the tonic Major 7#11 chord is sustained. Lydian sounds beautiful over a tonic sus 2 chord, for Example, A Lydian over Asus2

Example 14b:

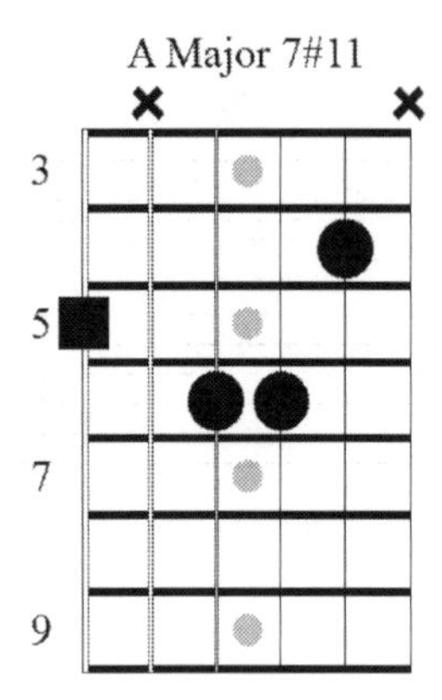

This chord accurately outlines the full harmony of the Lydian sound. It is worth noting that this voicing doesn't contain the 5th of the chord as the semitone clash between the 5th and the #11 is undesirable.

Another approach is to use upper structure triads over a bass note. Notice that chords I and II in Lydian are both Major. We can use those two chords together over a tonic bass note to create a rich, compelling harmony. For example:

Example 14c:

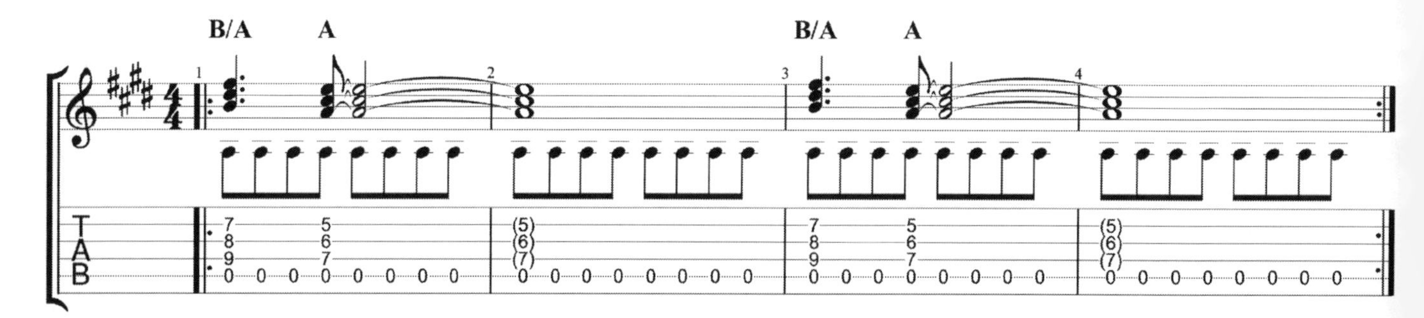

This is the approach that Joe Satriani takes in *Flying in a Blue Dream* by arpeggiating chord sequence in the key of C Lydian.

Due to the open, 'spacey' nature of the Lydian mode, it is often played over suspended chord vamps.

Example 14d:

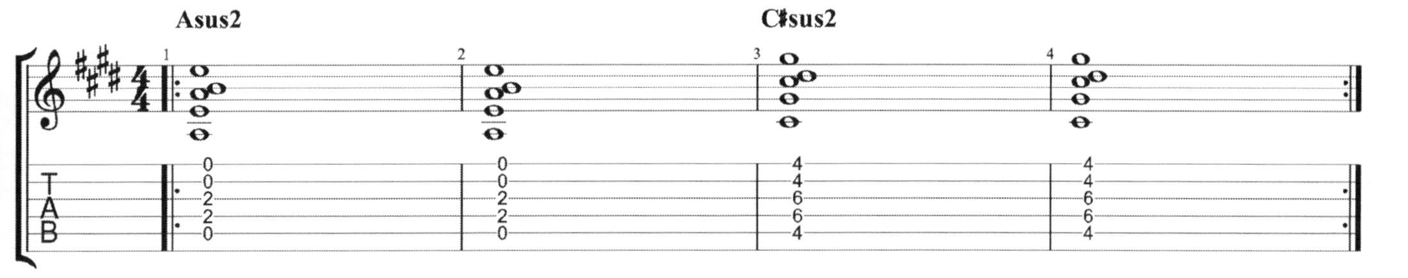

5 Useful Lydian Licks

These licks are all included as audio examples and the Lydian backing track has kindly been provided by **Quist**.

Example 14e:

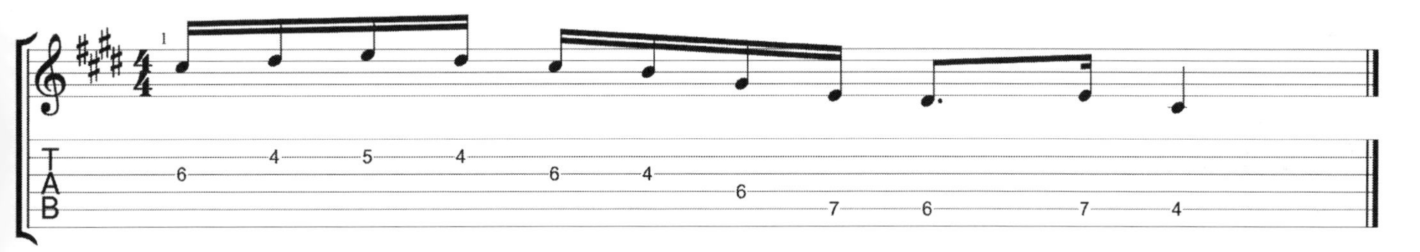

Example 14f:

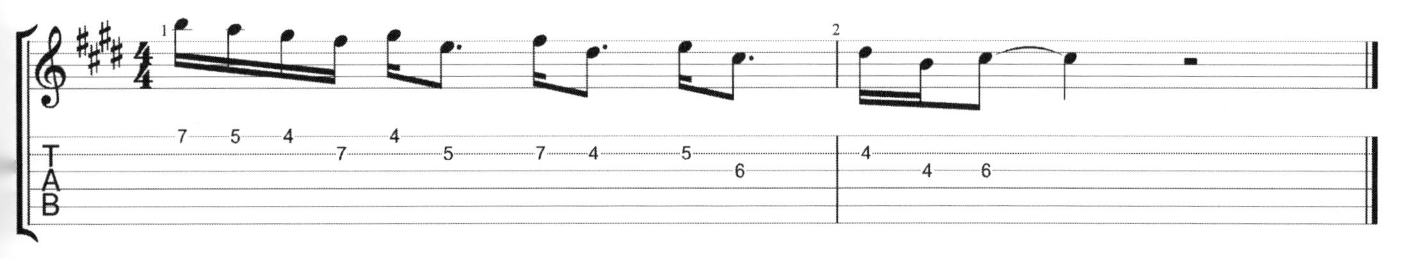

Example 14g:

Example 14h:

Example 14i:

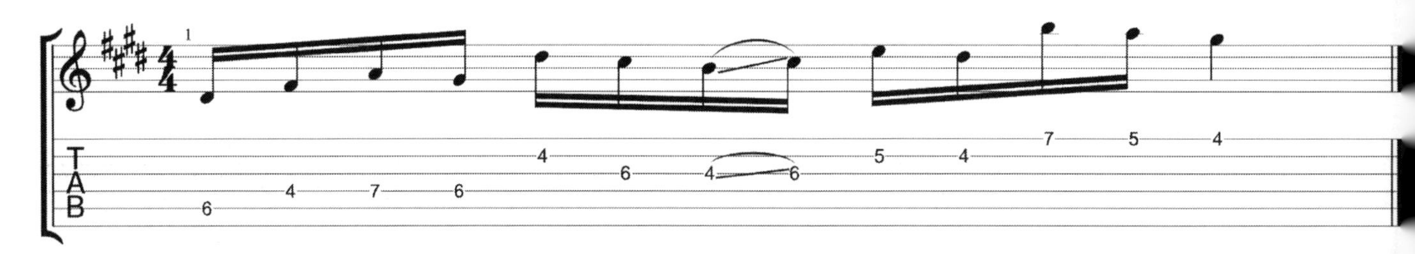

Soloing Approaches to the Lydian Mode

The following pages discuss the various structures in the Lydian mode, from 2-note intervals through to 5-note pentatonic scales. Any idea in the following section can be used as an isolated approach, or in combination with any other concept. Solo with these ideas and create your own melodies.

2-Note Intervals

Example 14j:

Example 14k:

Example 14l:

Example 14m:

Example 14n:

At first, I advise you to explore 3rds and 5ths. You can make melodic patterns out of groups of intervals. A common idea is to ascend two intervals and descend the third. Also, each interval pair can be played backwards.

3-Note Triads

We can isolate the individual triads that are built on each degree of the Lydian mode. By soloing with specific triads we can target or isolate particular scale tones while avoiding others. The triads built from the Lydian mode are:

Scale Degree	3-Note Triads Built in Lydian	Intervals Against Tonic
1	I Major	1, 3, 5
2	II Major	9, #11, 13
3	iii Minor	3, 5, 7
#4	#iv Minor b5	#11, 13, 1
5	V Major	5, 7, 9
6	vi Minor	13, 1, 3
7	vii Minor	7, 9, #11

As one octave shapes in the *first position,* they are played:

Example 14o:

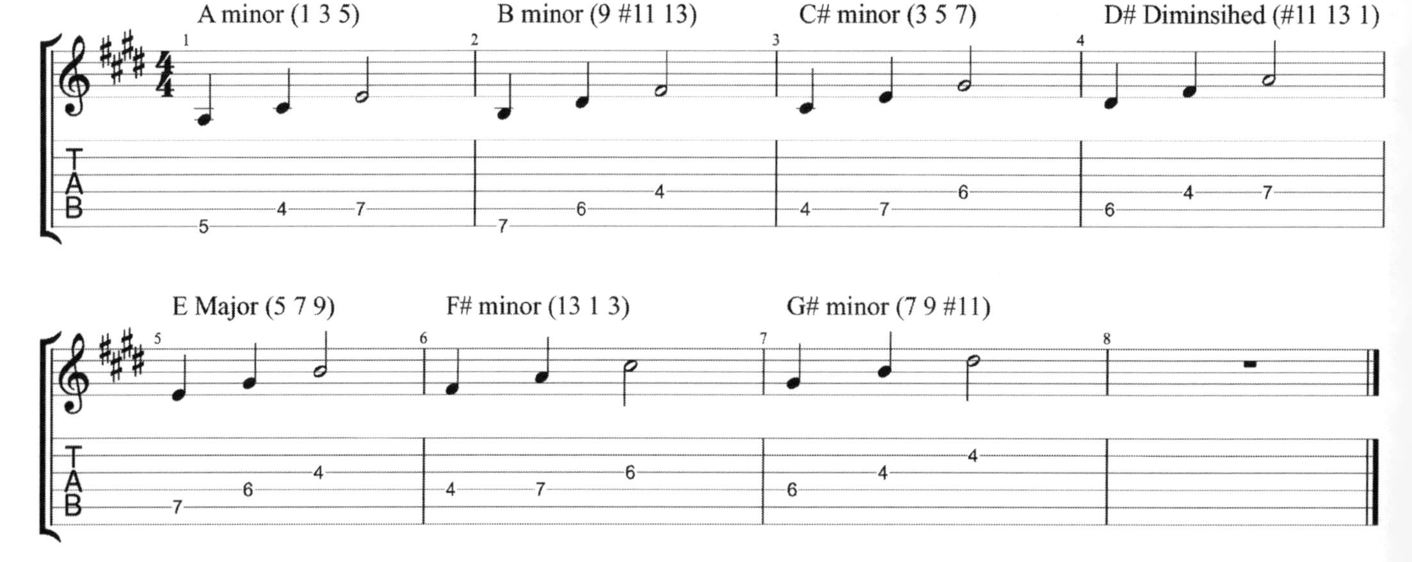

These can be played in two octaves in the following manner. (The lowest note in each shape is not always the root of the triad).

Example 14p:

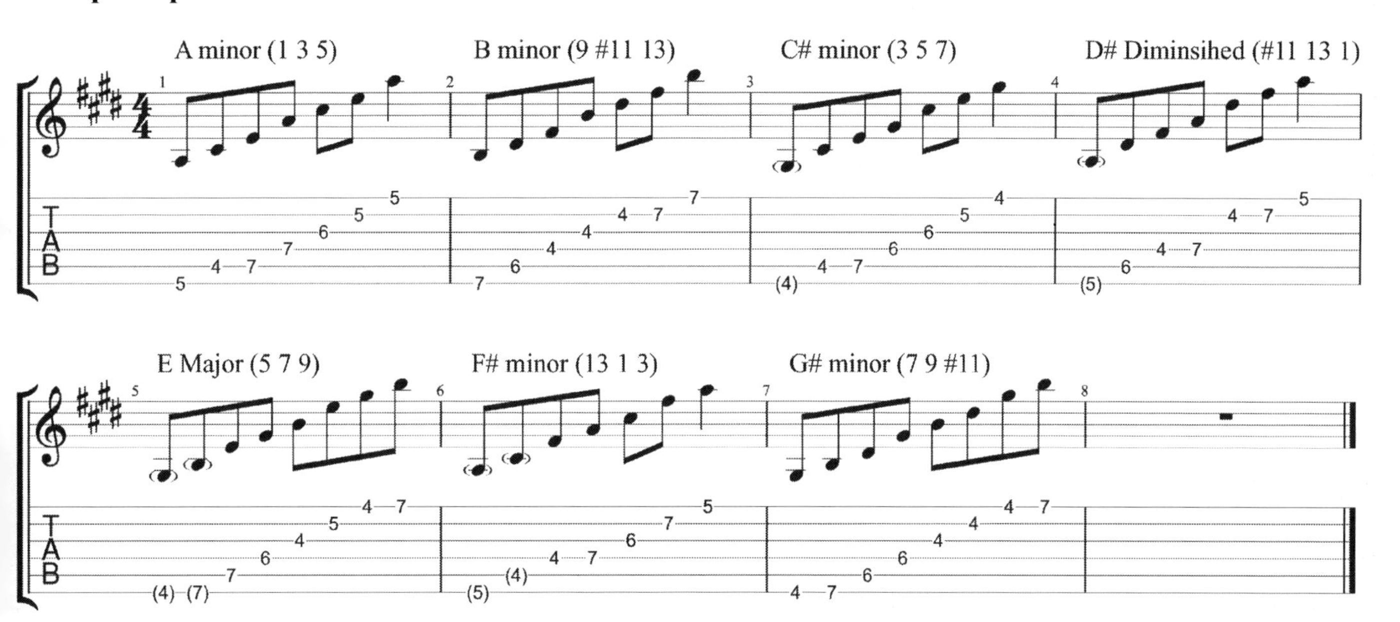

My favourite approaches are to play:

Minor triad on 7 (G# Minor over A Lydian) (7, 9, #11).

Minor triad on 3 (C# Minor over A Lydian) (3, 5, 7,).

4-Note Arpeggios

When we extend the triad to become a 4-note arpeggio we access another level of texture and intervallic selection. By using 4-note arpeggios we can be articulate about which notes we choose to play from a mode.

The arpeggios built from Lydian:

Scale Degree	4-Note Arpeggios in Lydian	Intervals Against Tonic
1	I Major 7	1, 3, 5, 7
2	II7	9, #11, 13, 1
3	iii Minor 7	3, 5, 7, 9
#4	#iv Minor 7b5	#11, 13, 1, 3
5	V Major 7	5, 7, 9, #11
6	vi Minor 7	13, 1, 3, 5
7	vii Minor 7	7, 9, #11, 13

These can be played in 2 octaves in the following manner. The lowest note in each shape is not always the root.

Example 14q:

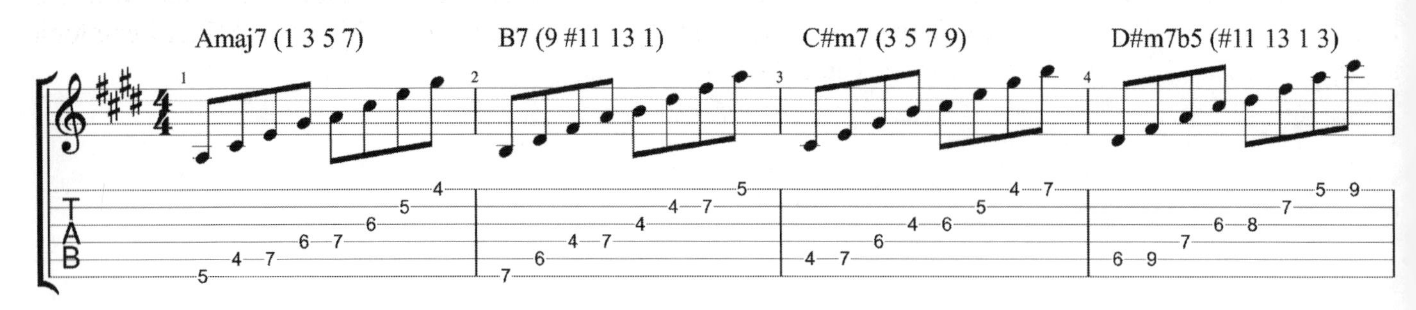

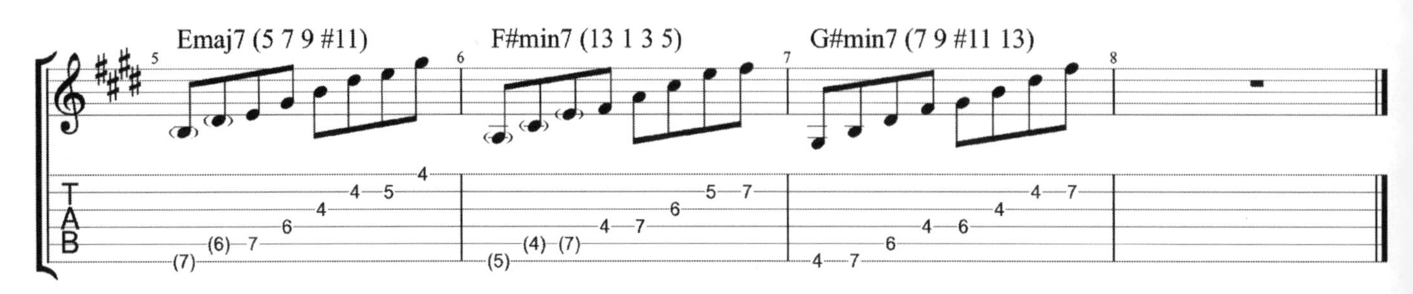

Two great choices are

Minor 7b5 on the #11th. (D#m7b5 over A Lydian) (#11, 13, 1, 3).

Minor 7 on the 3rd (C# Minor 7 over A Lydian) (3, 5, 7, 9).

5-Note Pentatonic Scales

It is extremely common to superimpose Minor Pentatonic scales over a Lydian mode chord sequence. These can be built on the 3rd, 7th and 13th (6th) degrees of the scale. To highlight the Lydian #11 use a Minor Pentatonic scale build on the 7th degree of the mode. The options are

Example 14r: Minor Pentatonic on 3:

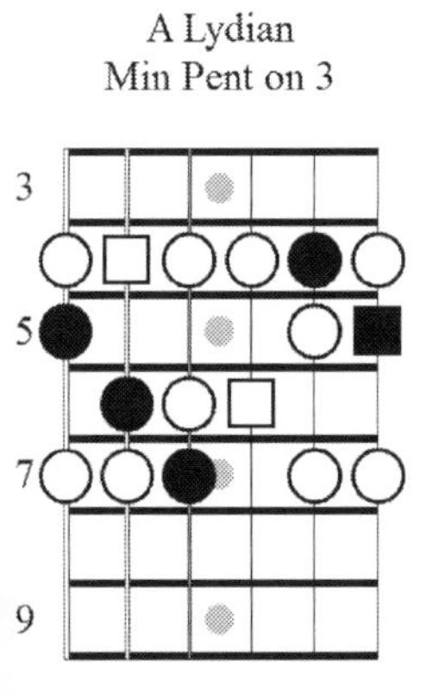

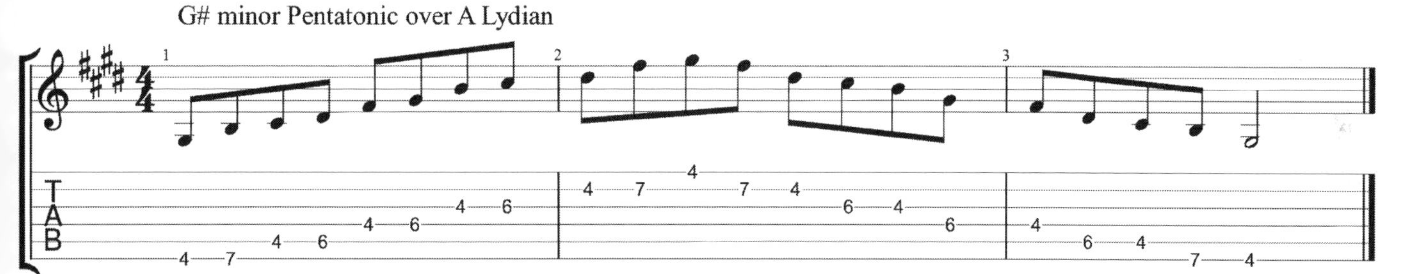

Intervals played against the root of Lydian: **3, 5, 13, 7, 9**.

Example 14s: Minor Pentatonic on 7:

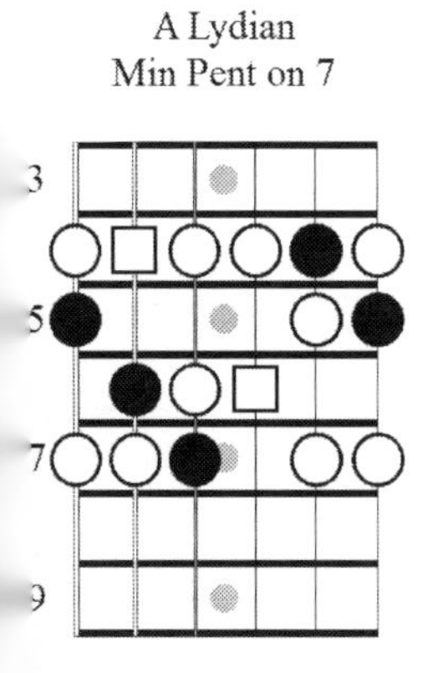

Intervals played against the root of Lydian: **3, 7, 9, #11, 13**.

Example 14t: Minor Pentatonic on 13/6:

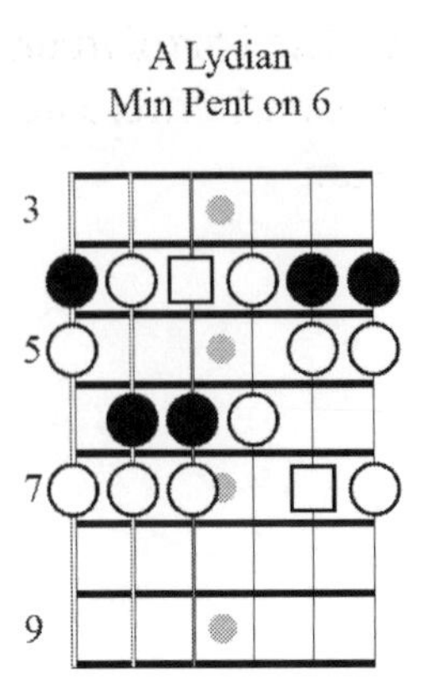

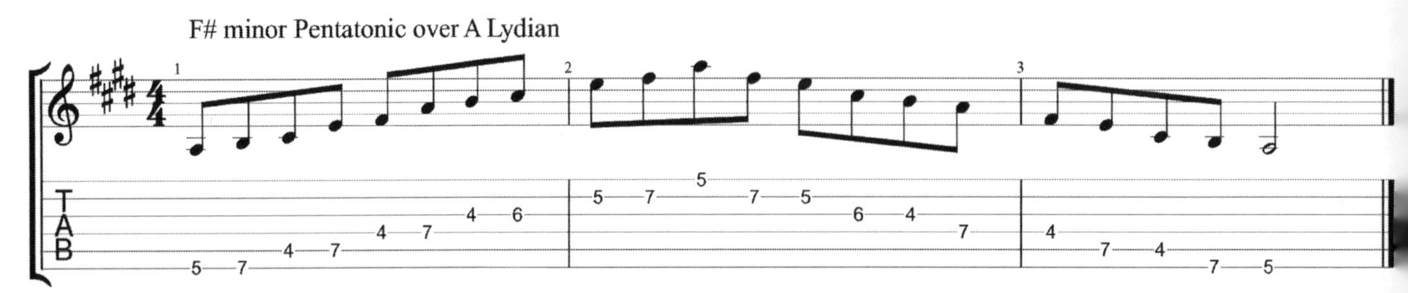

Intervals played against the root of Lydian: **1, 3, 5, 9, 13**.

My first choice is to play the Minor Pentatonic on the 7th (G# Minor Pentatonic over A Lydian) (7, 9, 3, #11 13).

First Choice Soloing Summary for the Lydian Mode

Parent Scale: Lydian

Intervals: 3rds and 5ths

Triads: Minor triad on 7 / Minor triad on 3

Arpeggio: Minor 7b5 on #11th / Minor 7 on 3

Pentatonic: Minor Pentatonic on the 7

Mixolydian

Mixolydian is built on the 5th degree of the Major scale and is one of the most frequently used modes in modern guitar playing. It is used to construct chord sequences and solos in a variety of musical styles. The Mixolydian mode, just like Lydian, contains only one note that is different from the Major scale, but that small difference creates a dramatically different mood. Mixolydian is in the roots of modern blues, rock, and funk.

It can be heard in a wide variety of popular music:

- **Sweet Child of Mine** – Guns and Roses
- **Sweet Home Alabama** – Lynyrd Skynyrd
- **Ramblin' Man** – The Allman Brothers Band
- **Summer Song** – Joe Satriani
- **Freeway Jam** – Jeff Beck

Formula and Harmonisation

The formula for the Mixolydian mode is **1 2 3 4 5 6 b7**

Visualise the Mixolydian mode around the Dominant 7 chord highlighted by hollow dots.

Example 15a:

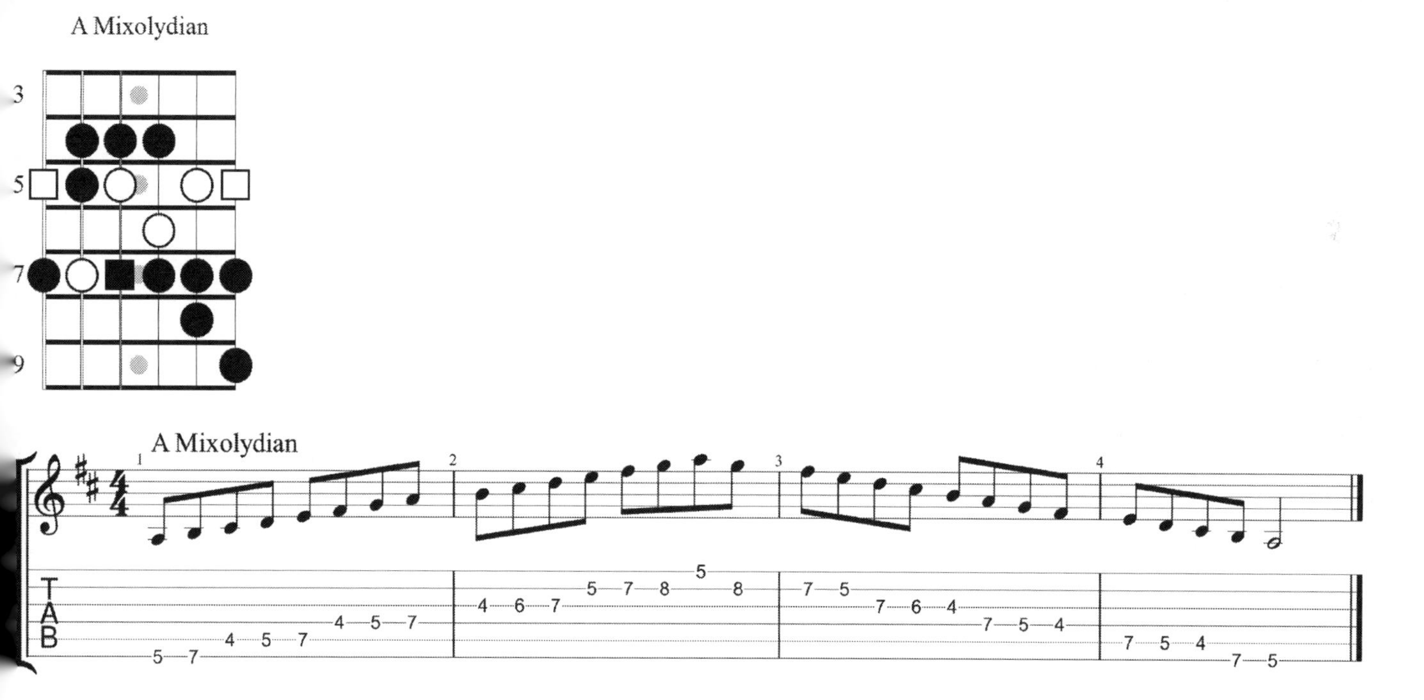

Mixolydian is harmonised to generate the following sequence of chords:

TRIAD Chord Type	SEVENTH Chord Types	Example in the key of A Mixolydian
I Major	I7 (extensions 9, 11, 13)	A7
ii Minor	ii Minor 7 (extensions 9, 11, b13)	B Minor 7
iii Minor b5	iii Minor 7b5 (extensions b9, 11, b13)	C# Minor 7b5
IV Major	IV Major 7 (extensions 9, 11, 13)	D Major 7
v Minor	V Minor 7 (extensions 9, 11, 13)	E Minor 7
vi Minor	vi Minor 7 (extensions b9, 11, b13)	F# Minor 7
bVII Major	bVII Major (extensions 9, #11, 13)	G Major 7

One of the most important things to know about the Mixolydian mode is that Chord I forms a Dominant 7 chord when it is harmonised to 4 notes. In classical music this is always seen as a point of tension which needs to be resolved. However, for about the last 100 years, the dominant chord has become a chord that can remain static indefinitely. For example, every chord in blues can be played as a dominant 7 chord.

A quick way to spot a Mixolydian riff is to see if it includes a bVII Major chord at any point. If the riff is major-sounding and it contains a bVII chord it is generally Mixolydian.

Typical Mixolydian Chord Progressions

Example 15b:

A Mixolydian A7 | D Mixolydian D7 | A Mixolydian A7

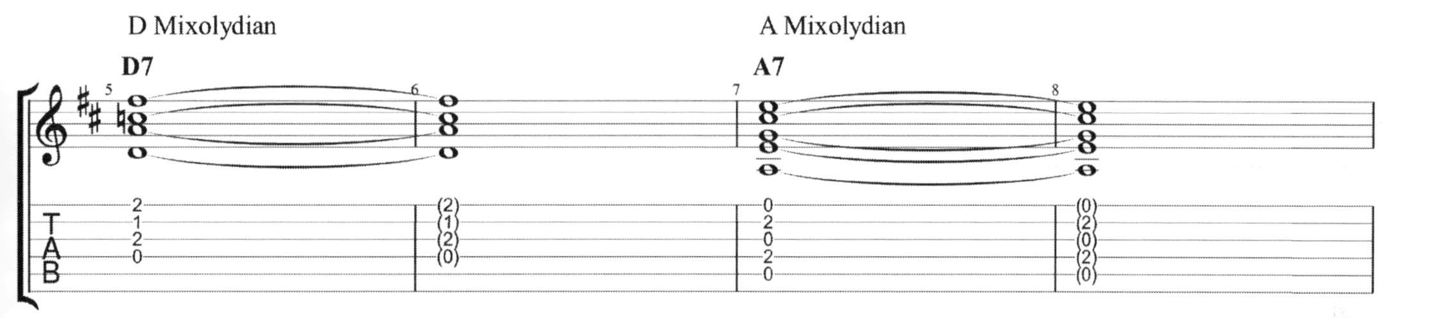

E Mixolydian E7 | D Mixolydian D7 | A Mixolydian A7 | E Mixolydian E7

Example 15c:

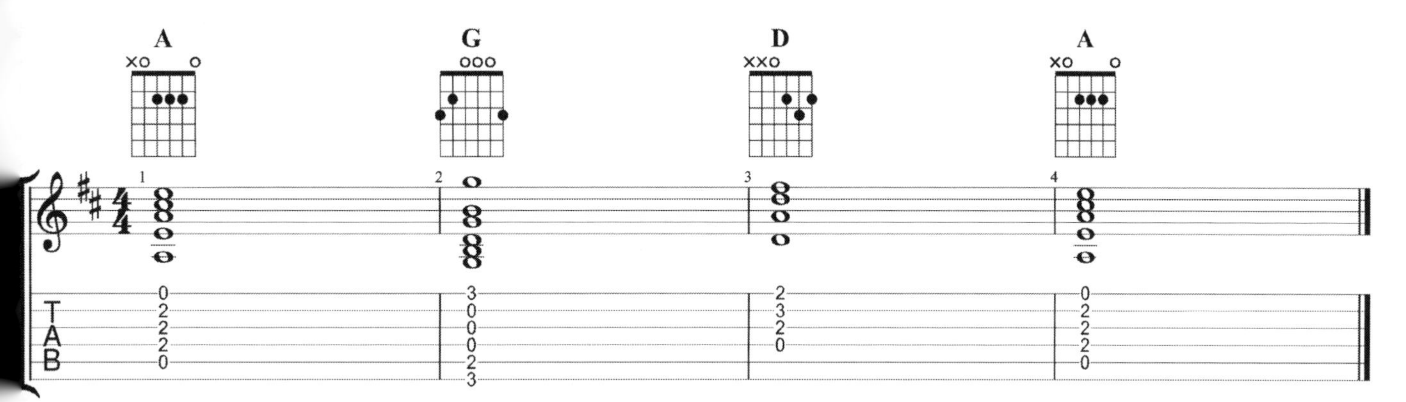

5 Useful Mixolydian Licks

Mixolydian is often added to the Minor Pentatonic and Blues scales to give a slightly happier lift to a blues solo. This is reflected in many of the licks in this section. They are all included as audio examples.

Example 15d:

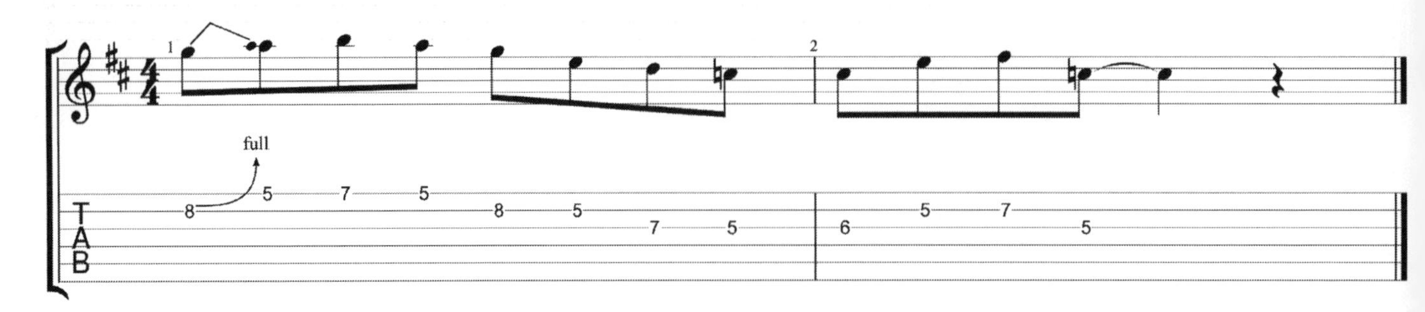

Example 15e:

Example 15f:

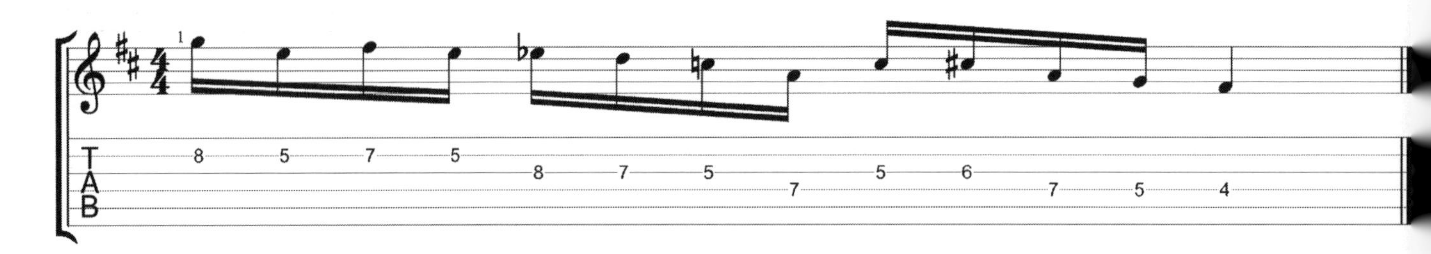

Example 15g:

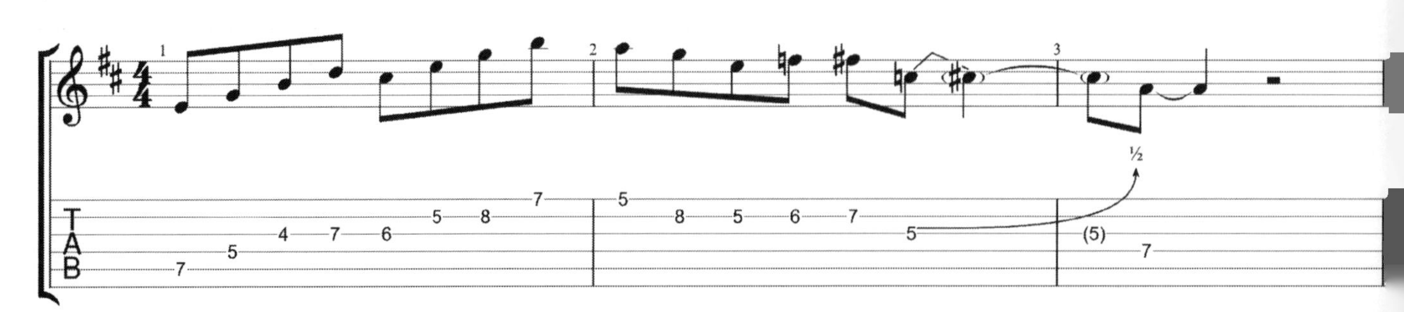

Example 15h:

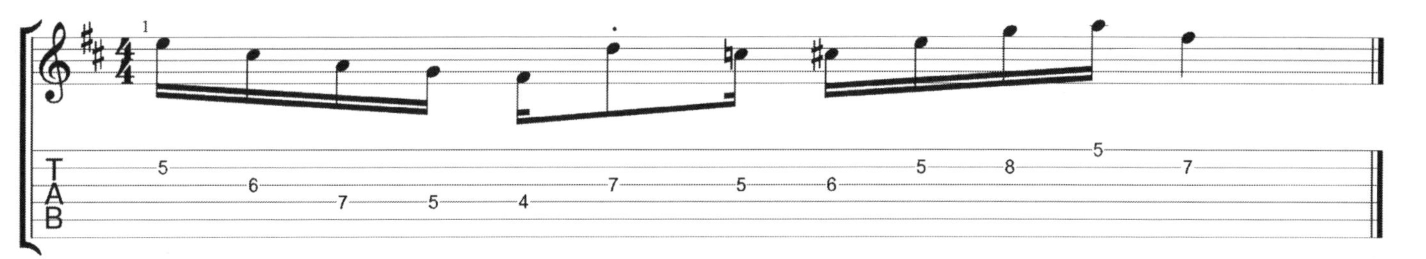

Soloing Approaches to the Mixolydian Mode

The following pages analyse the approaches we can use to dissect the A Mixolydian mode. Each approach, (intervals, triads etc.) represents one level of depth we can investigate to create melodies.

All the ideas can be freely combined in order to make a solo. Try each idea over a slow Mixolydian backing track to get a feel for the texture of each melodic concept.

2-Note Intervals

You should be comfortable playing all these Mixolydian intervallic approaches.

Example 15i:

Example 15j:

Example 15k:

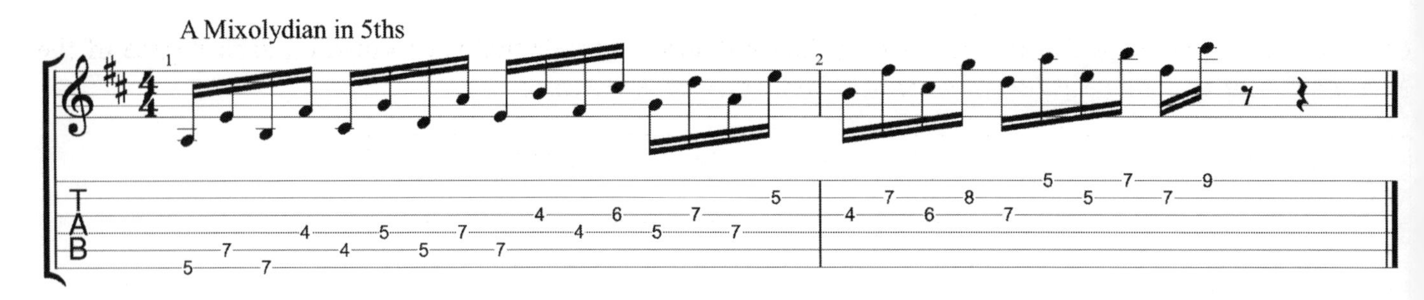

Example 15l:

Example 15m:

3-Note Triads

Once again, we can take the approach of singling out specific triads that are formed on each degree of the Mixolydian mode. The triads that are formed from each scale tone are:

Scale Degree	3-Note Triads Built in Mixolydian	Intervals Against Tonic
1	I Major	1, 3, 5
2	ii Minor	9, 11, 13
3	iii Minor b5	3, 5, b7
4	IV Major	11, 13, 1
5	v Minor	5, b7, 9
6	vi Minor	13, 1, 3
b7	bVII Major	b7, 9, 11

These are played in the following manner in one and two octaves:

Example 15n:

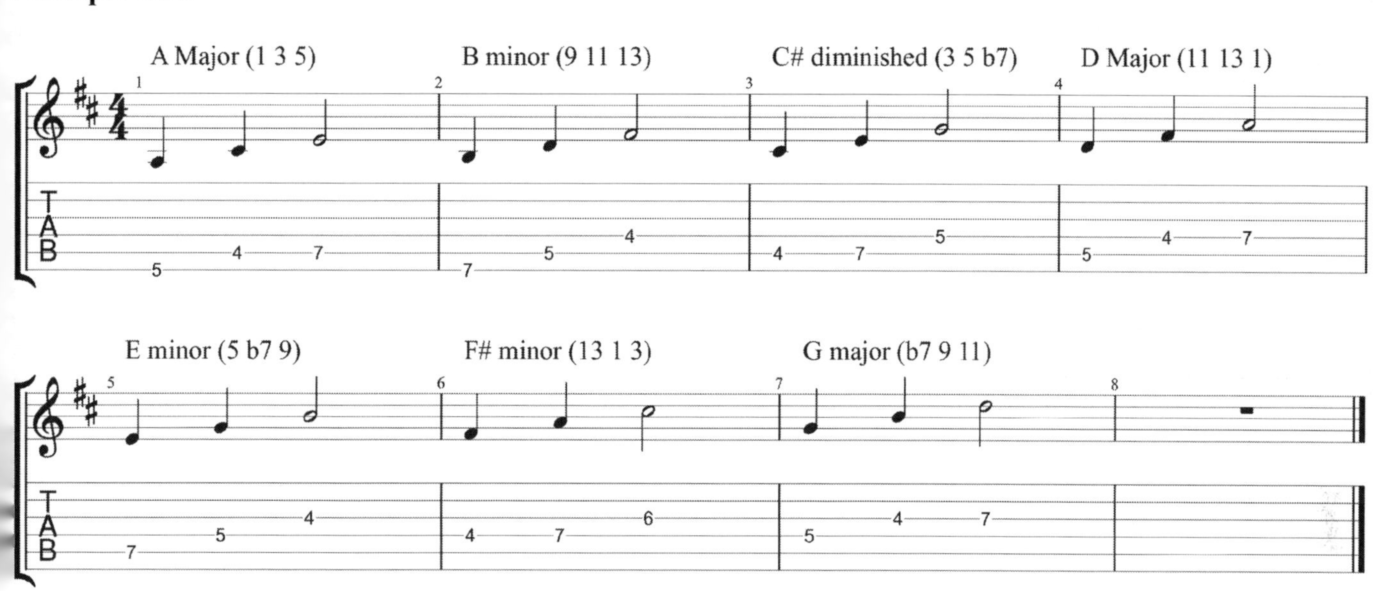

Example 15o:

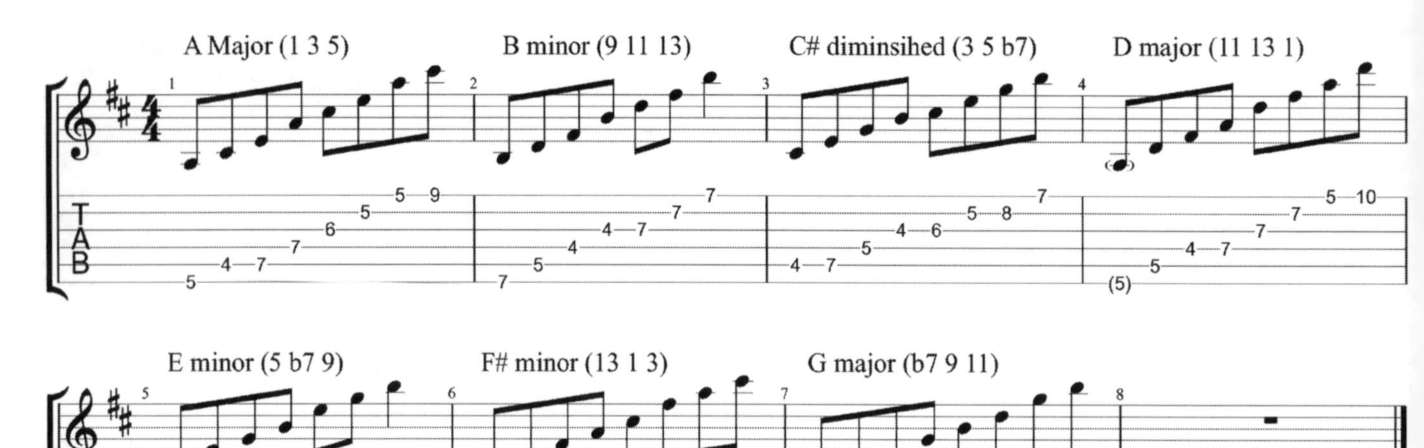

E minor (5 b7 9) F# minor (13 1 3) G major (b7 9 11)

Playing a Minor triad on the 5th degree of the Mixolydian mode is a great sound. (E Minor over A Mixolydian) (5, b7, 9).

4-Note Arpeggios

Building a 4-note arpeggio from each degree of Mixolydian generates the following soloing options:

Scale Degree	4-Note Arpeggios in Mixolydian	Intervals Against Tonic
1	I7	1, 3, 5, b7
2	ii Minor 7	9, 11, 13, 1
3	iii Minor 7b	3, 5, b7, 9
4	IV Major 7	11, 13, 1, 3
5	V Minor 7	5, b7, 9, 11
6	vi Minor 7	13, 1, 3, 5
b7	bVII Major	b7, 9, 11, 13

Example 15p:

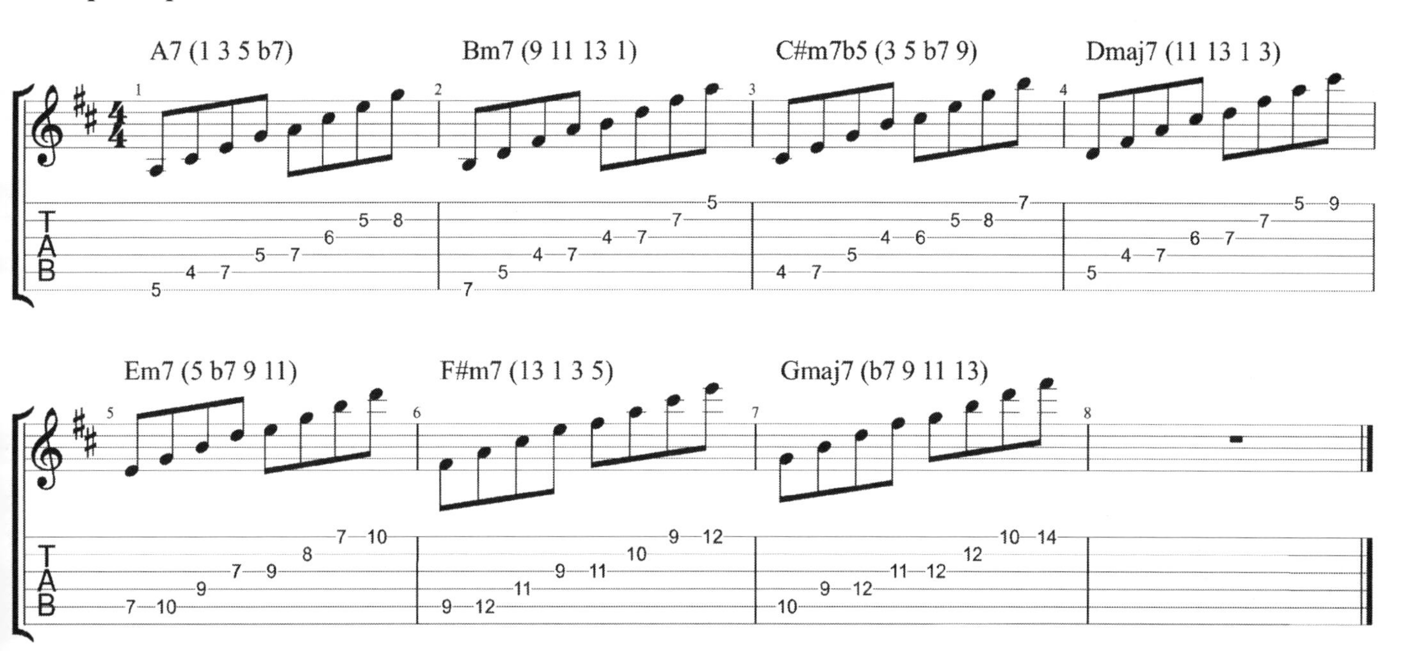

Common approaches include playing a Minor 7b5 arpeggio from the 3rd. (C#m7b5 over A Mixolydian) (3, 5, b7, 9).

Playing a Minor 7 arpeggio from the 5th (E Minor 7 over A Mixolydian) (5, b7, 9, 11) works well too.

5-Note Pentatonic Scales

Minor Pentatonic scales are often combined with the Mixolydian mode to create a rocky, bluesy feel. Despite the Mixolydian mode being a *Major*-type mode (it contains a major 3rd), the most common Minor Pentatonic scale to use it with is built from the *root* and This would contain a *minor* 3rd.

For example, an A Minor Pentatonic scale is often used in conjunction with the A Mixolydian mode. A large part of blues vocabulary involves bending the minor 3rd of the pentatonic toward the major 3rd in Mixolydian. Many rock guitar licks begin as Minor Pentatonic lines and then ‘borrow’ notes from Mixolydian to create a slightly happier vibe.

Examine the following line:

Example 15q:

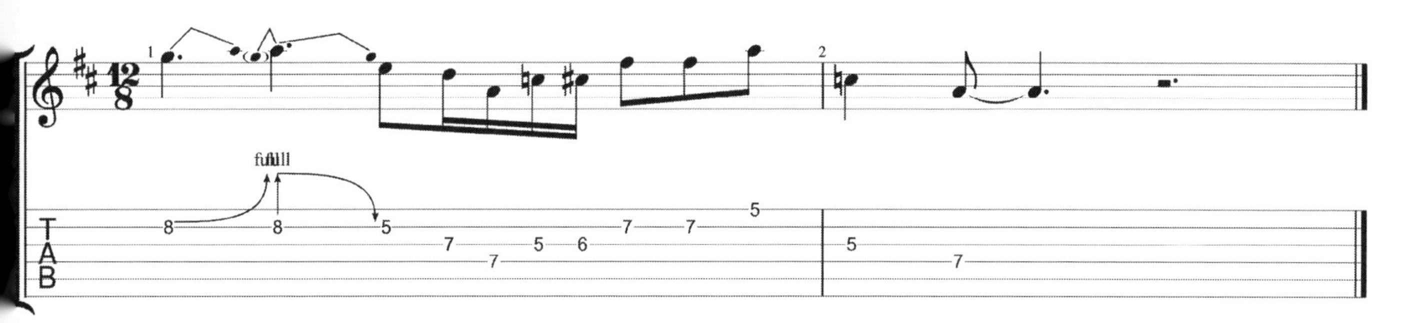

This line begins as an A Minor lick, but borrows some notes from A Mixolydian in beats 2 and 3. Joe Satriani, Stevie Ray Vaughan and Jimi Hendrix are great players who all use this idea.

While the Minor Pentatonic scale from the root is not an organic derivative of the Mixolydian mode, it is probably the most commonly used approach when soloing in a rock/blues context.

The Minor Pentatonic scales that exist naturally in the Mixolydian mode are built on the 5th, 6th (13th) and 2nd (9th).

Example 15r: Minor Pentatonic on 5:

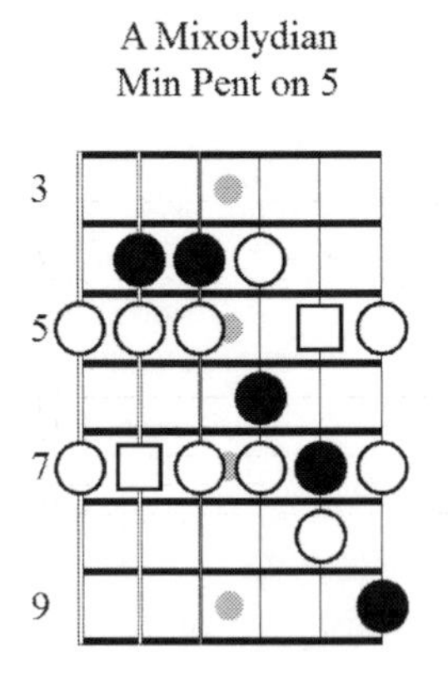

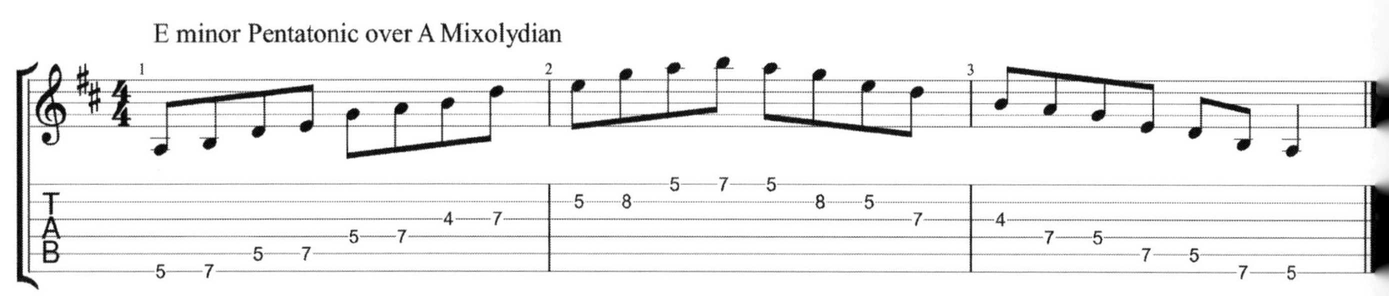

Intervals played against the root of Mixolydian: **1, 5 b7, 9, 11**.

Example 15s: Minor Pentatonic on 6/13:

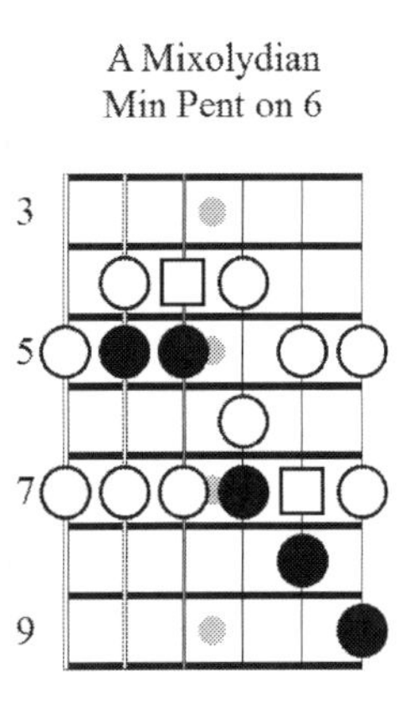

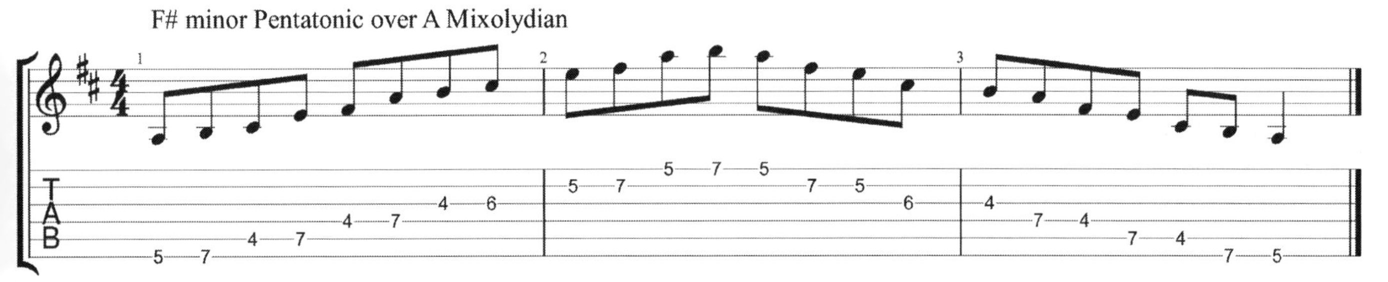

Intervals played against the root of Mixolydian: **1, 3, 5, 9, 13**.

Example 15t: Minor Pentatonic on 9:

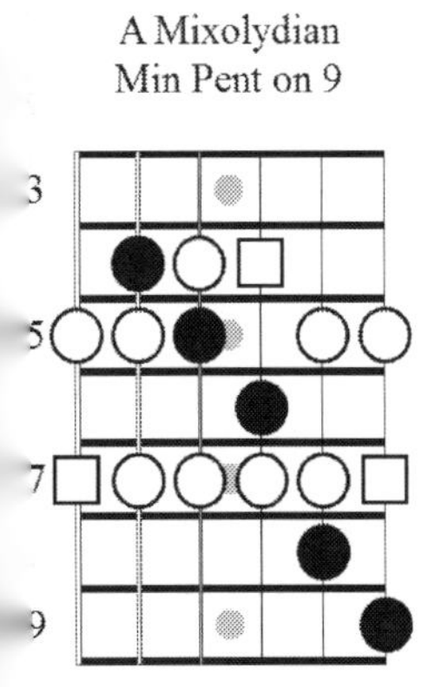

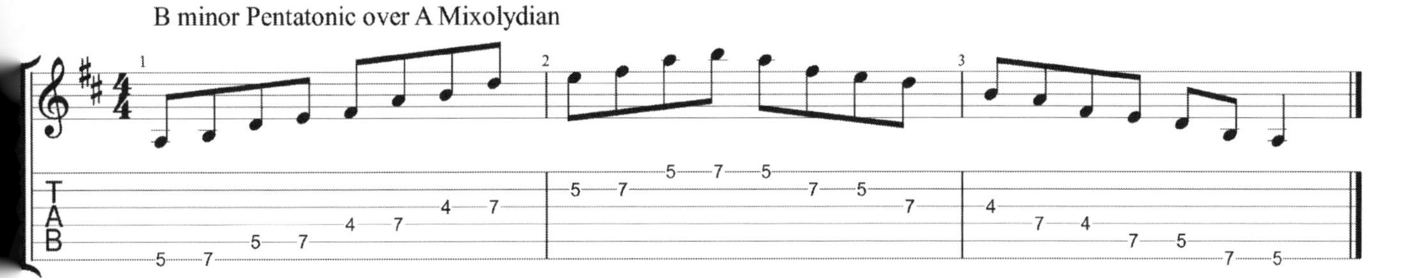

Intervals played against the root of Mixolydian: **1, 5, 9, 11, 13**.

If we include the Minor Pentatonic scale from the root (A Minor Pentatonic), the *Mixolydian mode contains two pairs of Minor Pentatonic scales, both one tone apart.*

For example, in A Mixolydian:

We have: A Minor and B Minor Pentatonics. (Minor Pentatonic on root and 9)

And E Minor and F# Minor Pentatonics. (Minor Pentatonic on 5 and 6)

In other words, you can shift any E Minor Pentatonic lick or idea up one tone to F#, or any A Minor Pentatonic idea up by a tone to play B Minor Pentatonic of A Mixolydian.

First Choice Soloing Summary for the Mixolydian Mode

Parent Scale: Mixolydian.

Intervals: 3rds and 6ths.

Triad: Minor triad on 5.

Arpeggio: Minor 7b5 on 3 / Minor 7 on 5.

Pentatonic: Minor Pentatonic on 5 / Minor Pentatonic on the 1.

Aeolian

The Aeolian mode is formed by building a scale from the 6th degree of the Major scale and is identical to the natural or relative Minor scale. It is a dark and foreboding sound and is used frequently in rock and metal guitar solos. Some notable compositions that use Aeolian are:

- **Still Got the Blues** – Gary Moore
- **Europa** – Carlos Santana
- **All Along the Watchtower** – Bob Dylan
- **Losing my Religion** – R.E.M.
- **Fear of the Dark** – Iron Maiden

Formula and Harmonisation

The formula for the Aeolian mode is **1 2 b3 4 5 b6 b7**

Example 16a:

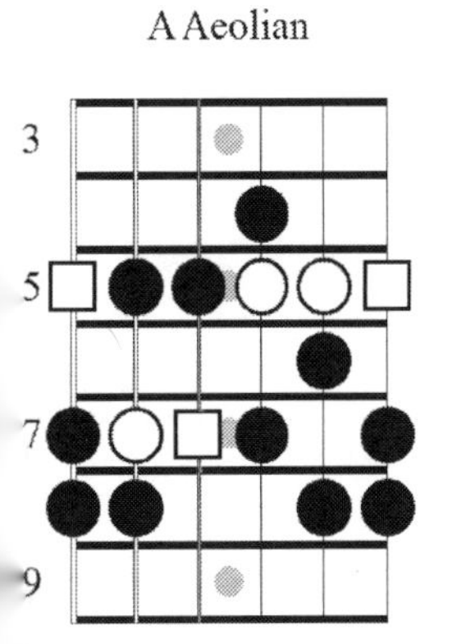

It is useful to visualise this scale around the tonic Minor chord highlighted by hollow dots.

The Aeolian mode, when harmonised forms the following sequence of chords:

TRIAD Chord Type	SEVENTH Chord Types	Example in the key of A Aeolian
i Minor	i Minor 7 (extensions 9, 11, b13)	A Minor 7
ii Minor b5	ii Minor 7b5 (extensions b9, 11, b13)	B Minor 7b5
bIII Major	III Major 7 (extensions 9, 11, 13)	C Major 7
iv Minor	iv Minor 7 (extensions 9, 11, 13)	D Minor 7
v Minor	v Minor 7 (extensions b9, 11, b13)	E Minor 7
bVI Major	bVI Major7 (extensions 9, #11, 13)	F Major 7
bVII Major	bVII 7 (extensions 9, 11, 13)	G7

Notice that the important and key-defining i, iv and v chords are all minor. This lends a dark quality to the mode.

A chord progression that includes a shift to the bVI (Major) chord is typically Aeolian.

Chord bVII will tend to be played as a major triad and not as a dominant 7 because the dominant tension pulls the progression strongly towards the relative major key, (in this case C Major).

Typical Aeolian Chord Progressions

Example 16b:

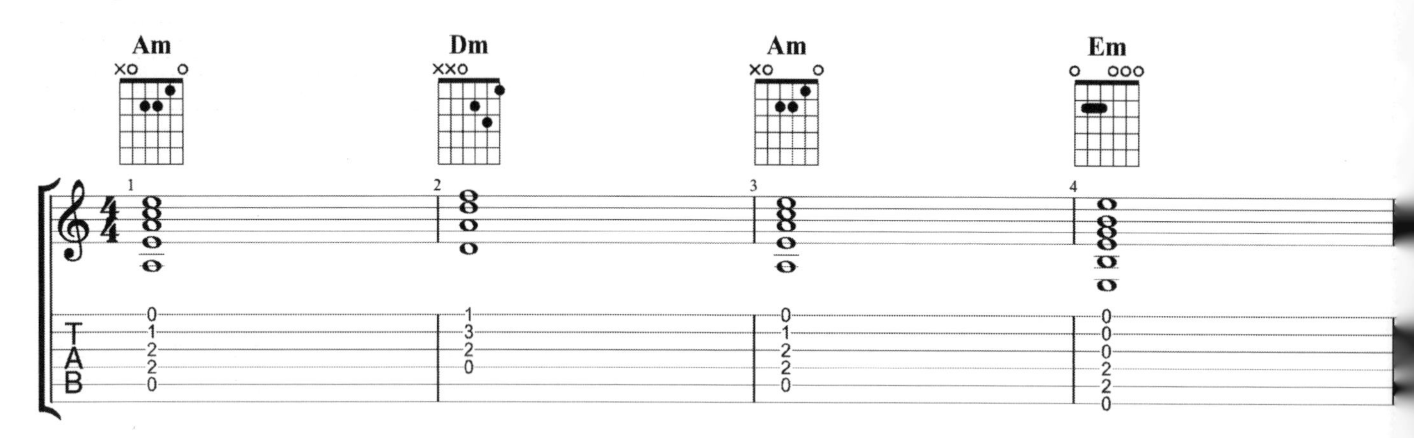

Example 16c:

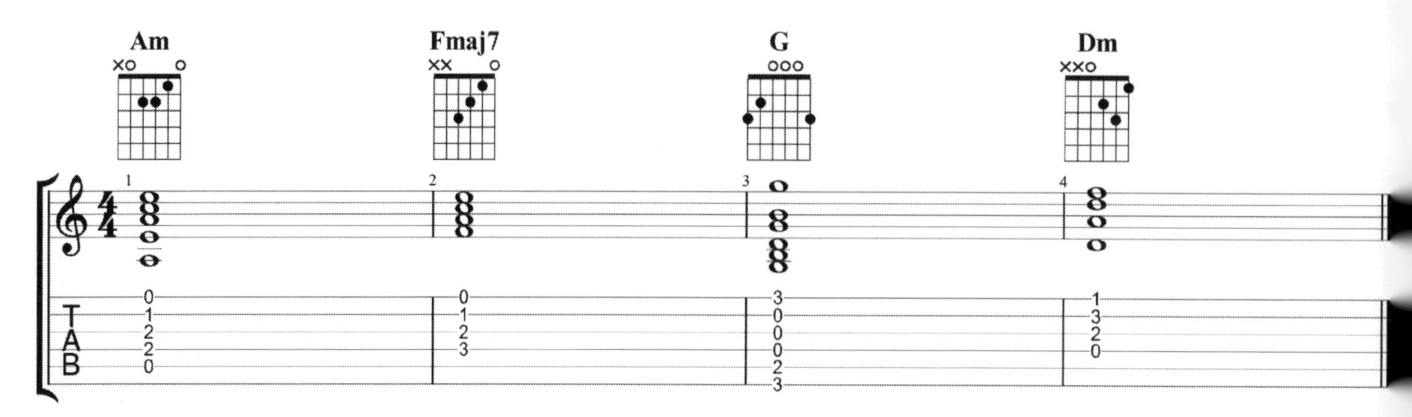

Example 16d:

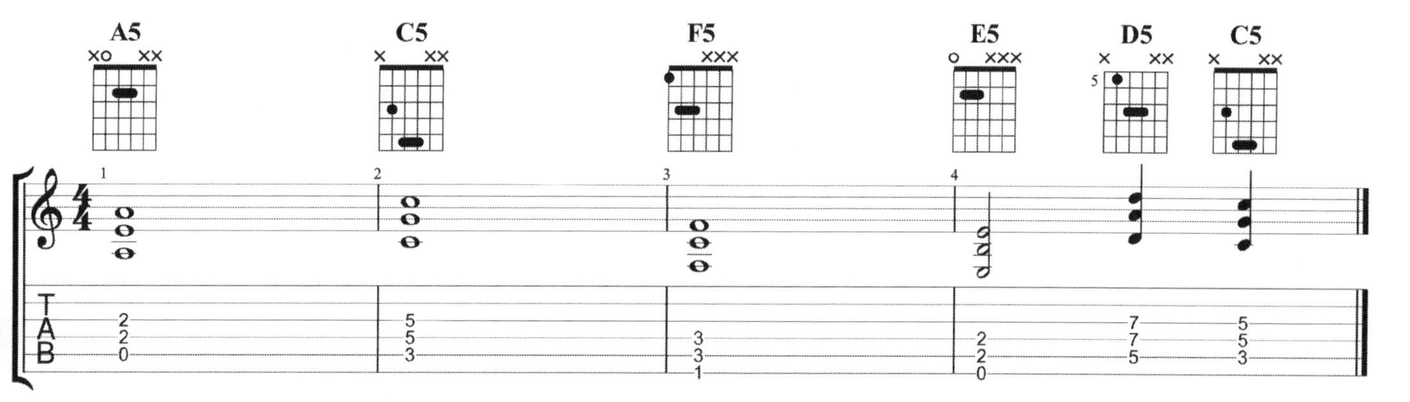

5 Useful Aeolian Licks

The following licks will get you into the Aeolian sound. Use them with the corresponding backing track.

Example 16e:

Example 16f:

Example 16g:

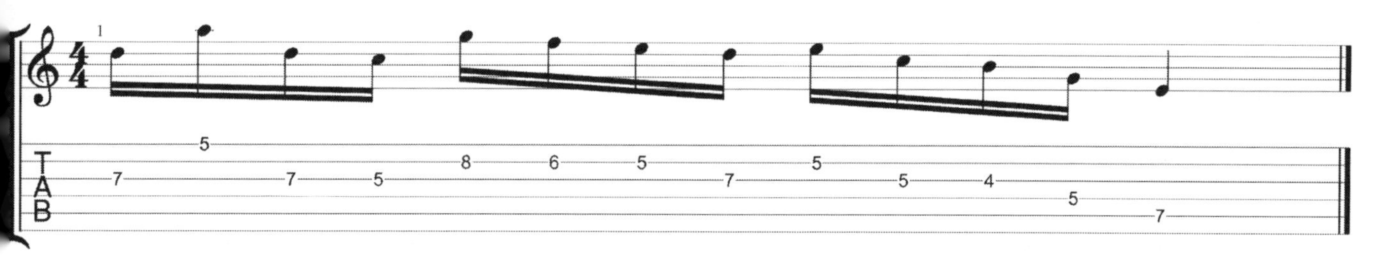

Example 16h:

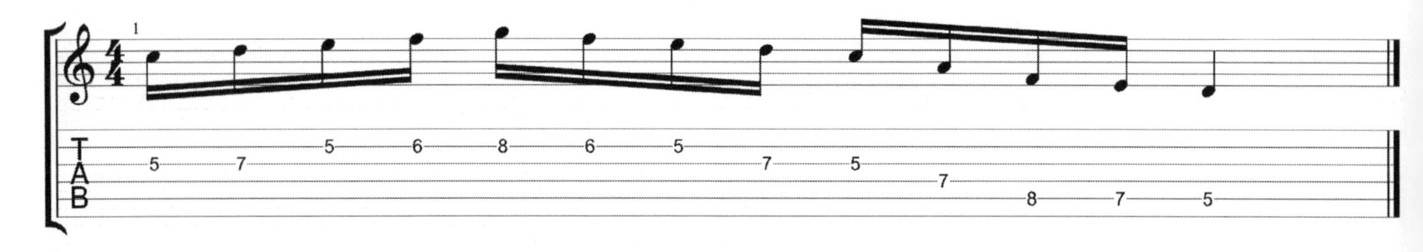

Example 16i:

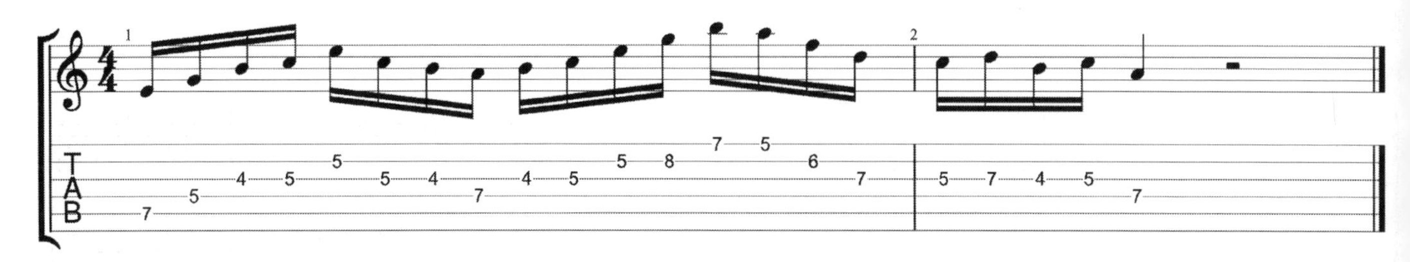

Soloing Approaches to the Aeolian Mode

The following section dissects the Aeolian mode into various soloing approaches; from soloing using 2-note intervals, right through to exploring the 5-note Minor Pentatonic scales which exist on three degrees of the scale. With these approaches, you will fuel your own improvisational fluency while securing important theoretical concepts.

2-Note Intervals

Example 16j:

Example 16k:

Example 16l:

Example 16m:

Example 16n:

While all these intervallic options sound good, I tend to play a lot of ideas based around **3rds and 4ths.**

3-Note Triads

When we form triads on each degree of the Aeolian mode, the following soloing opportunities are presented:

Scale Degree	3-Note Triads Built in Aeolian	Intervals Against Tonic
1	i Minor	1, b3, 5
2	ii Minor b5	9, 11, b13
b3	bIII Major	b3, 5, b7
4	iv Minor	11, b13, 1
5	v Minor	5, b7, 9
b6	bVI Major	b13, 1, b3
b7	bVII Major	b7, 9, 11

Each triad when played in isolation imposes a different set of extensions over the tonal centre. One and two octave patterns are shown in the following examples along with the extensions they form against the tonic.

Example 16o:

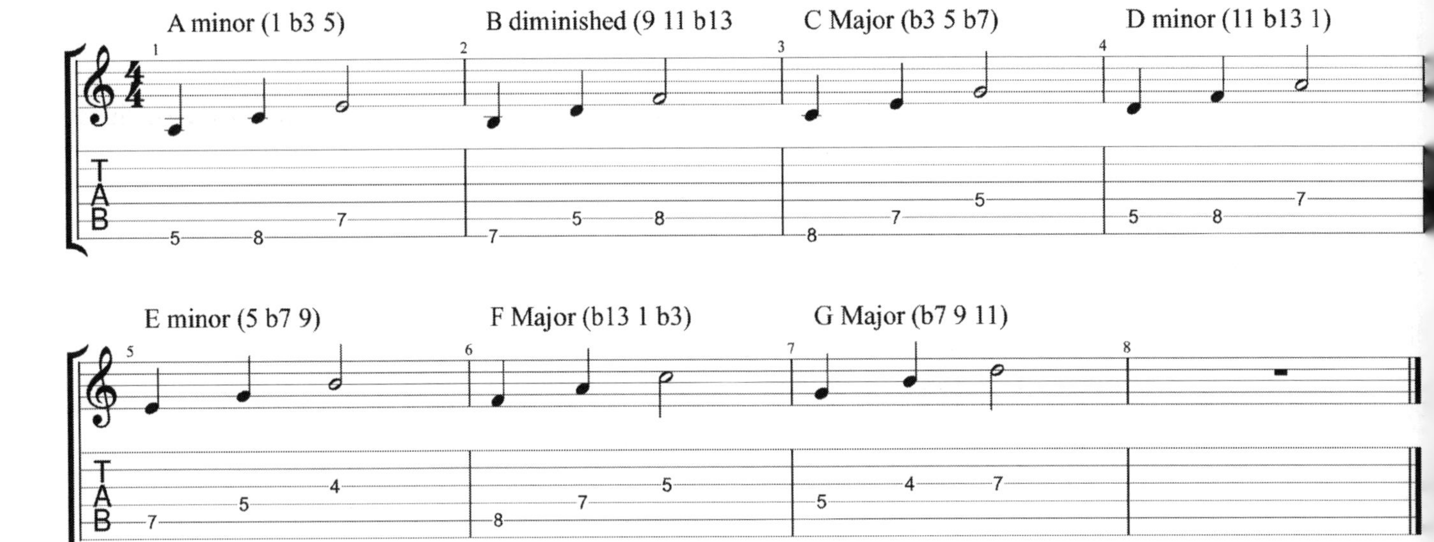

Example 16p:

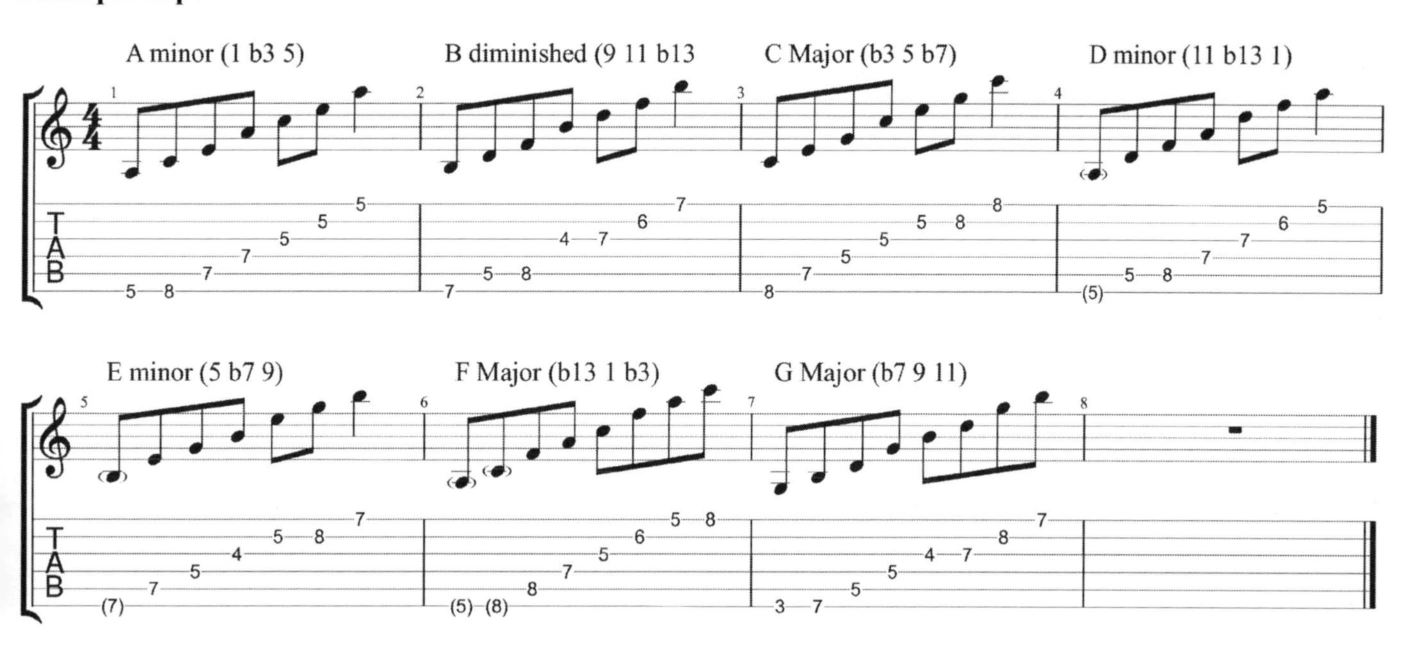

There are plenty of good options here, but I would suggest that you start by exploring the Major triad on the b6, (F Major over A) (1, b3, b13).

4-Note Arpeggios

The arpeggios derived from each scale tone are as follows:

Scale Degree	4-Note Arpeggios built in Aeolian	Intervals Against Tonic
1	i Minor 7	1, b3, 5, b7
2	ii Minor 7b5	9, 11, b13, 1
b3	III Major 7	b3, 5, b7, 9
4	iv Minor 7	11, b13, 1, b3
5	v Minor 7	5, b7, 9, 11
b6	bVI Major7	b13, 1, b3, 5
b7	bVII 7	b7, 9, 11, b13

Example 16q:

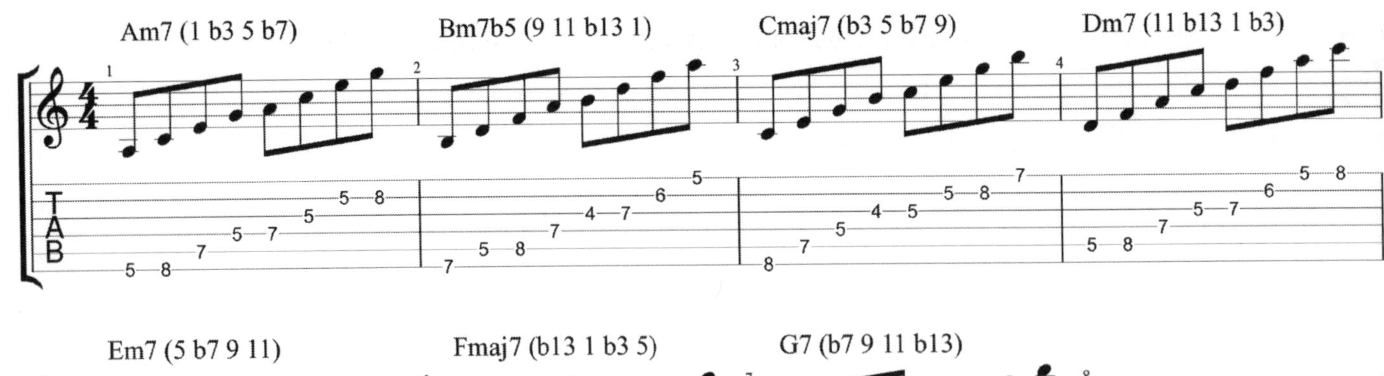

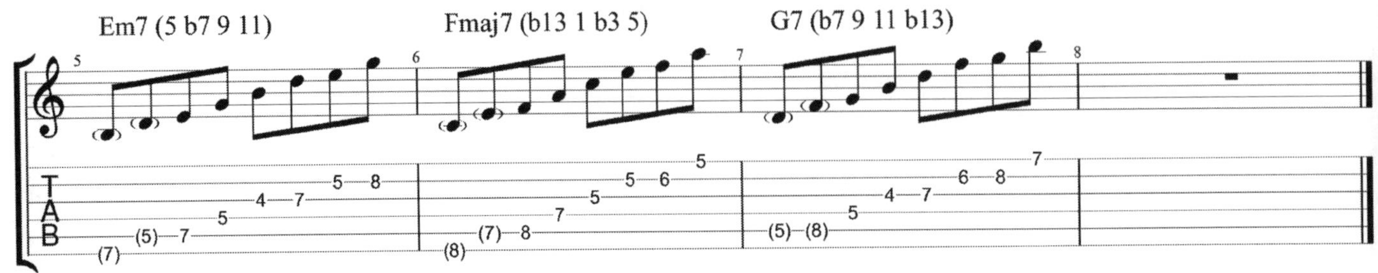

Two great arpeggios you can use to outline the Aeolian tonality are

Major 7th arpeggio on the b3 (C Major 7 over A) (b3, 5, b7, 9).

Minor 7th arpeggio on the 4th/11th (D Minor 7 over A) (1, b3, 11, b13).

5-Note Pentatonic Scales

Minor Pentatonic scales can be formed on the root, 11th and 5th of the Aeolian mode.

Example 16r: Minor Pentatonic on 1:

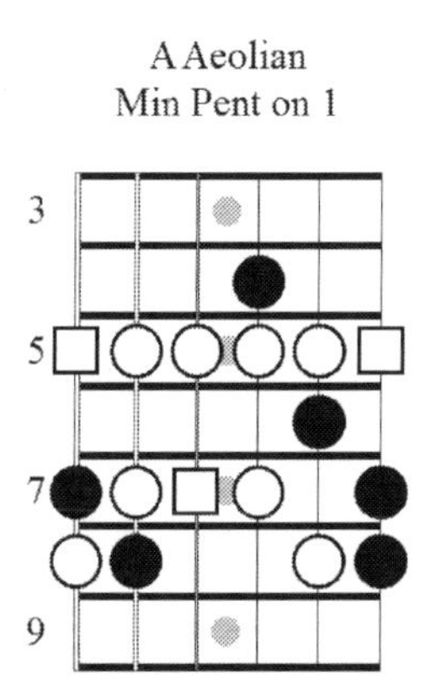

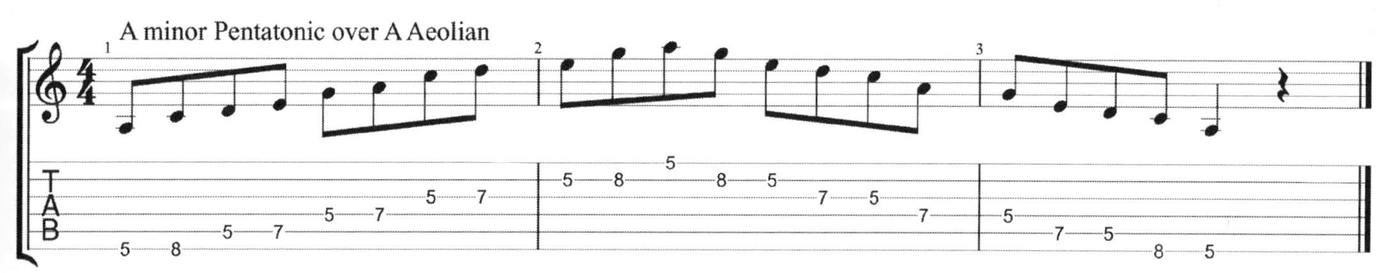

Intervals played against the root of Aeolian: **1, b3, 4, 5, b7.**

Example 16s: Minor Pentatonic on 11/4:

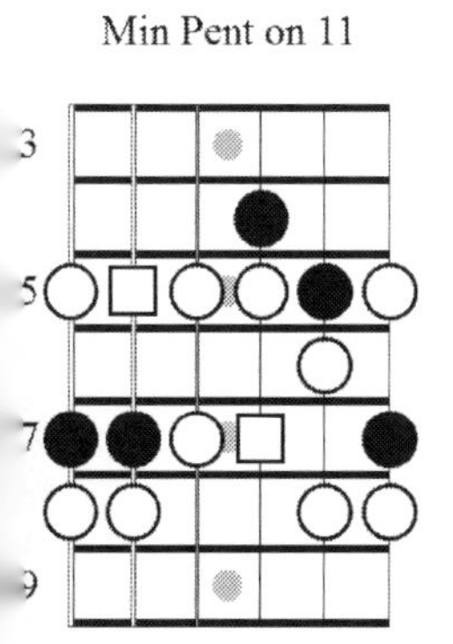

Intervals played against the root of Aeolian: **1, b3, b7, 11, b13.**

Example 16t: Minor Pentatonic on 5:

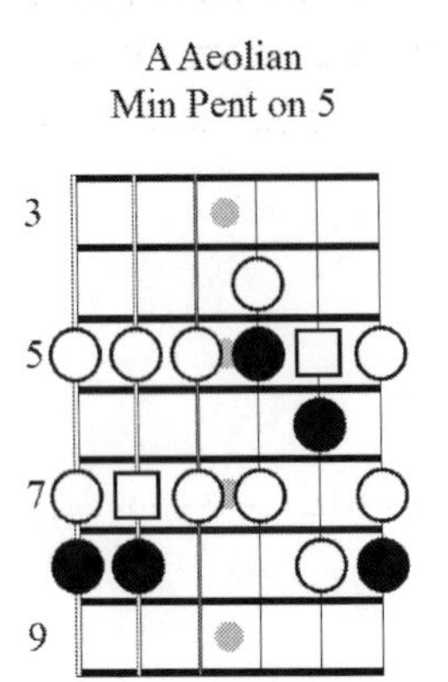

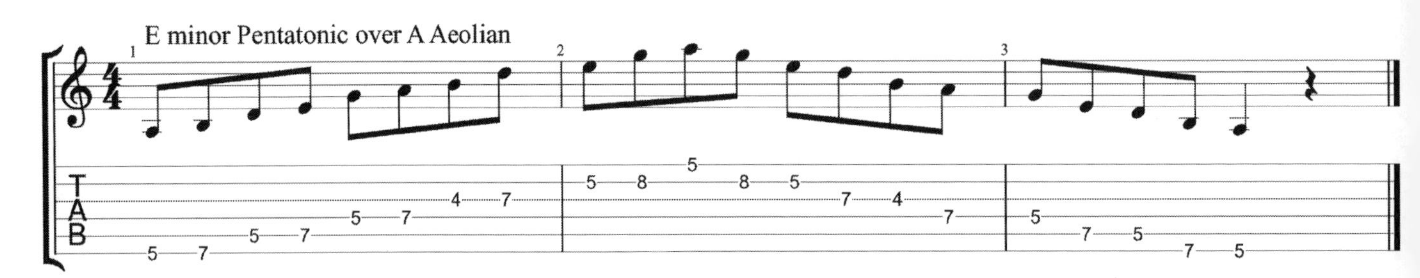

Intervals played against the root of Aeolian: **1, 5, b7, 9, 11.**

Playing Minor Pentatonic scales on the 4th and 5th degrees of Aeolian are both good soloing options.

First Choice Soloing Summary for the Aeolian Mode

Parent Scale: Aeolian.

Intervals: 3rds and 4ths.

Triad: Major triad on b6.

Arpeggio: Major 7th arpeggio on the b3 / Minor 7th arpeggio on the 4th.

Pentatonic: Minor Pentatonic on 4 and 5.

Locrian

Locrian is a rarely (read "never") used mode in pop and rock music, although it used over m7b5 chords in jazz. As the tonic (i) chord in Locrian harmonises to become a Minor 7b5 chord, the mode can sound extremely dark and unsettled because the tonic chord does not contain a perfect 5th. Pure Locrian as a key centre for soloing is also unusual. Spend your time learning Mixolydian, Dorian and Aeolian instead of Locrian.

Formula and Harmonisation

The formula for the Locrian mode is **1 b2 b3 4 b5 b6 b7**. Notice that every note except for the IV is flattened.

The highlighted chord below is an A Minor 7b5 (Am7b5).

Example 17a:

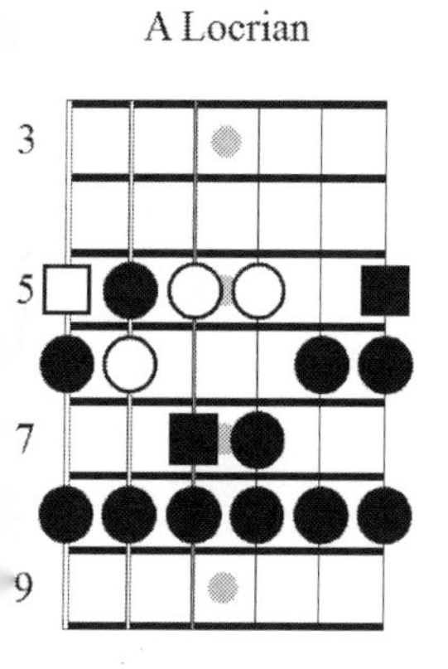

When harmonised, the Locrian mode generates the following sequence of chords:

TRIAD Chord Type	SEVENTH Chord Types	Example in the key of A Locrian
i Minor b5	i Minor 7b5 (extensions b9, 11, b13)	A Minor 7b5
bII Major	bII Major 7 (extensions 9, 11, 13)	Bb Major 7
biii Minor	biii Minor 7 (extensions 9, 11, 13)	C Minor 7
iv Minor	iv Minor 7 (extensions b9, 11, b13)	D Minor 7
bV Major	bV Major7 (extensions 9, #11, 13)	Eb Major 7
bVI Major	bVI 7 (extensions 9, 11, 13)	F7
bvii Minor	bvii Minor 7 (extensions 9, 11, b13)	G Minor 7

Locrian does *not* have a natural 5th degree. The V to I chord movement is important in stabilising a key centre, so the fact that it does not exist in Locrian explains partly why this mode is so unsettled.

Typical Locrian Chord Progressions

There is no such thing as a typical Locrian chord progression, however it can be implied by using *upper structure* chords over a bass note (slash chords). In its simplest form, this approach involves taking Major or Minor triads or 7th chords from the harmonised scale and playing them over a static bass note (normally the *root* of the key).

Example 17b:

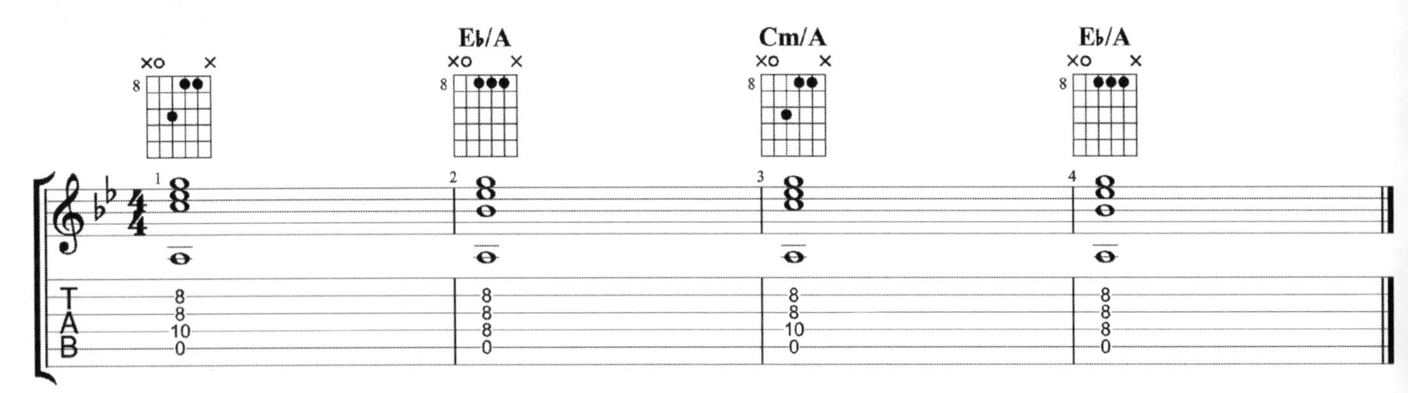

Example 17c:

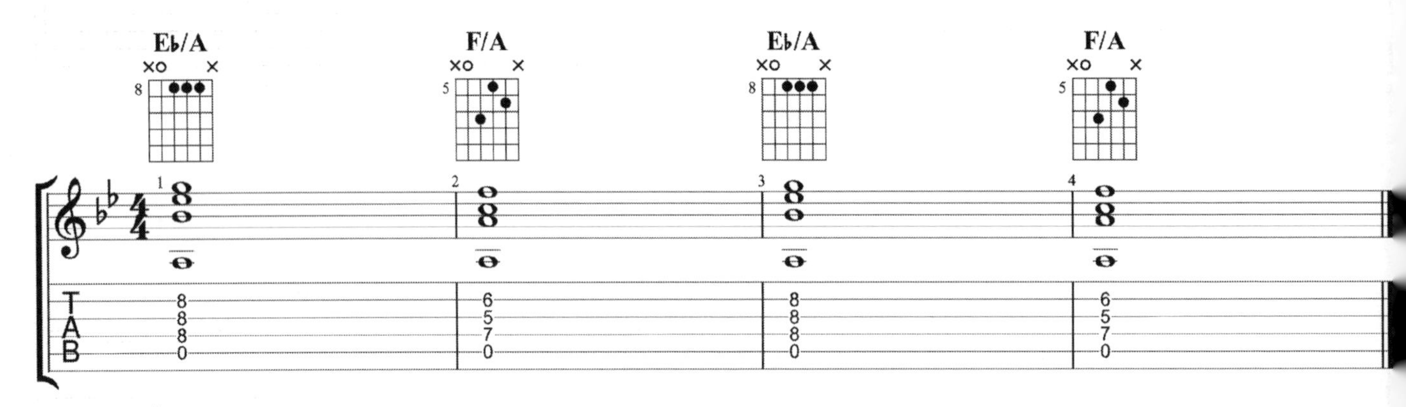

For more of a heavy metal feel, you can use power chords, but remember that chord i is played with a b5, rather than a natural 5 for a purer Locrian sound.

Example 17d:

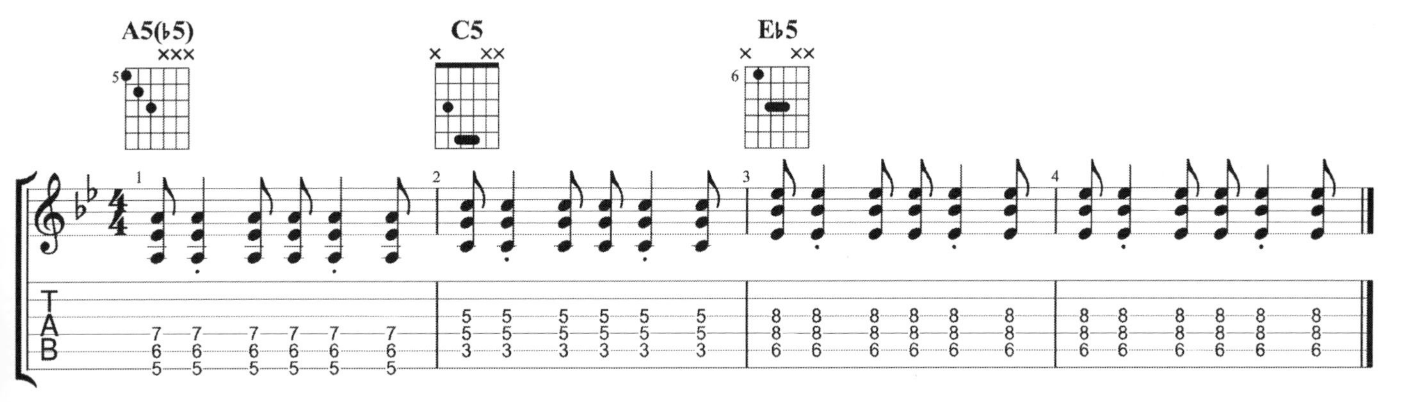

5 Useful Locrian Licks

These licks are all included as audio examples and the Locrian backing track has kindly been provided by **Quist**.

Example 17e:

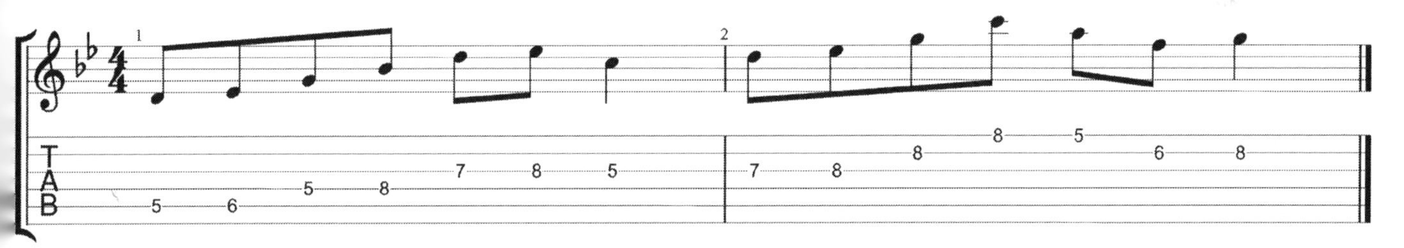

Example 17f:

Example 17g:

Example 17h:

Example 17i:

Soloing Approaches to the Locrian Mode

Once again, by extracting individual intervals, triads, arpeggios and pentatonic scales from the Locrian mode we can target specific scale degrees and articulately outline the Locrian sound.

2-Note Intervals

Example 17j:

Example 17k:

Example 17l:

Example 17m:

Example 17n:

Because of its dark nature, there are no bad options here. Use your ears and experiment. I tend to stick to 3rds and 4ths.

3-Note Triads

The harmonised Locrian created the following sequence triads:

Scale Degree	3-Note Triads Built in Locrian	Intervals Against Tonic
1	i Minor b5	1, b3, b5
b2	bII Major	b9, 11, b13
b3	biii Minor	b3, b5, b7
4	iv Minor	11, b13, 1
b5	bV Major	b5, b7, b9
b6	bVI Major	b13, 1, b3
b7	bvii Minor	b7, b9, 11

They are shown here with the Locrian scale degrees they give access to.

Example 17o:

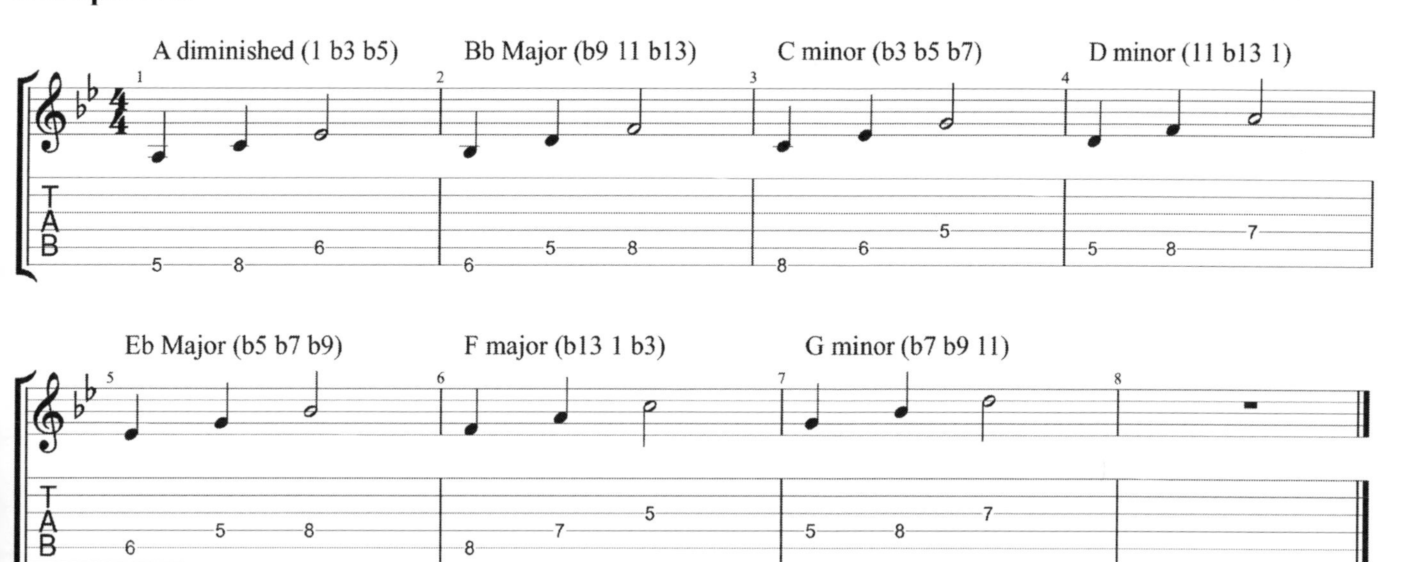

Example 17p:

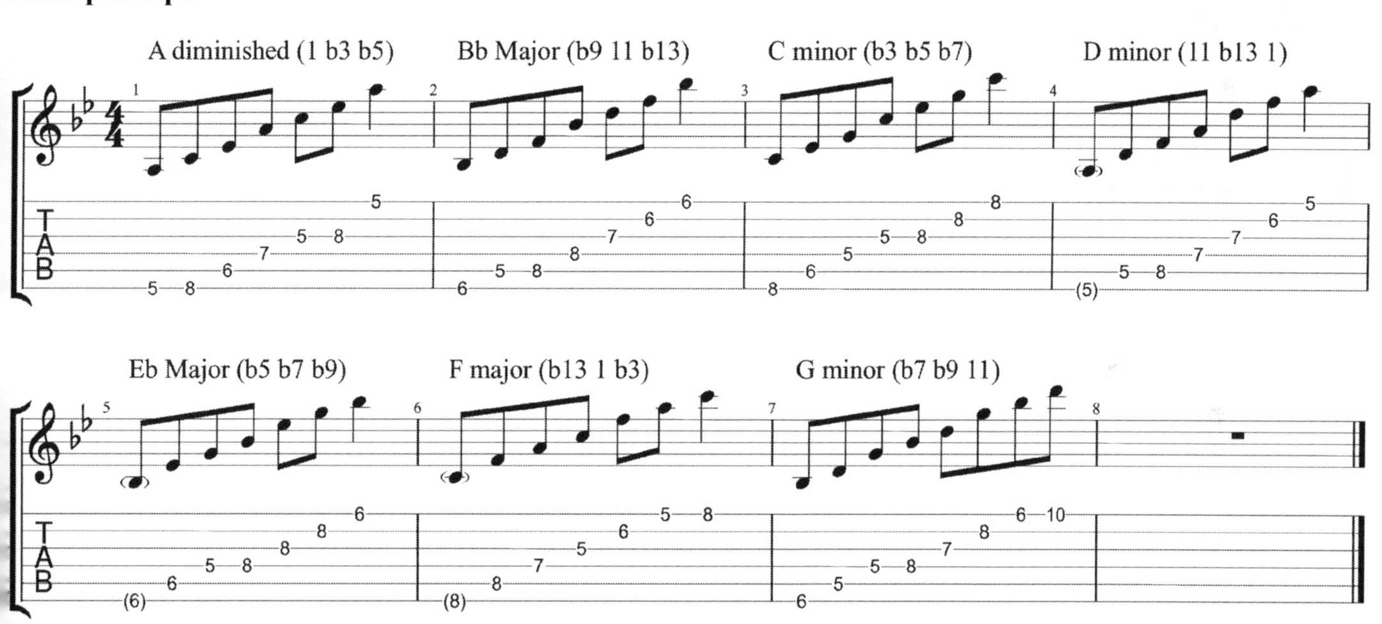

As any Locrian chord progression in going to be pretty dissonant, you can let the harmony do some of the work for you and stick to relatively 'safe' chord tones in your solos. Playing a Minor triad from the b3 (C Minor over A) would give you a safe set of chord tones (b3, b5, b7) but some good choices to emphasise the darkness of the mode would be

Major triad on the b5 (Eb Major over A) (b5, b7, b9).

Minor triad on the the b7 (G Minor over A) (b7, b9, 11).

4-Note Arpeggios

Extending the triads built on each scale degree to 4 note arpeggios generates the following soloing possibilities:

Scale Degree	4-Note Arpeggios built in Locrian	Intervals Against Tonic
1	i Minor 7b5	1, b3, b5, b7
b2	bII Major 7	b9, 11, b13, 1
b3	biii Minor 7	b3, b5, b7, b9
4	iv Minor 7	11, b13, 1, b3
b5	bV Major7	b5, b7, b9, 11
b6	bVI 7	b13, 1, b3, b5
b7	bvii Minor 7	b7, b9, 11, b13

Over two octaves they can be played in the following way.

Example 17q:

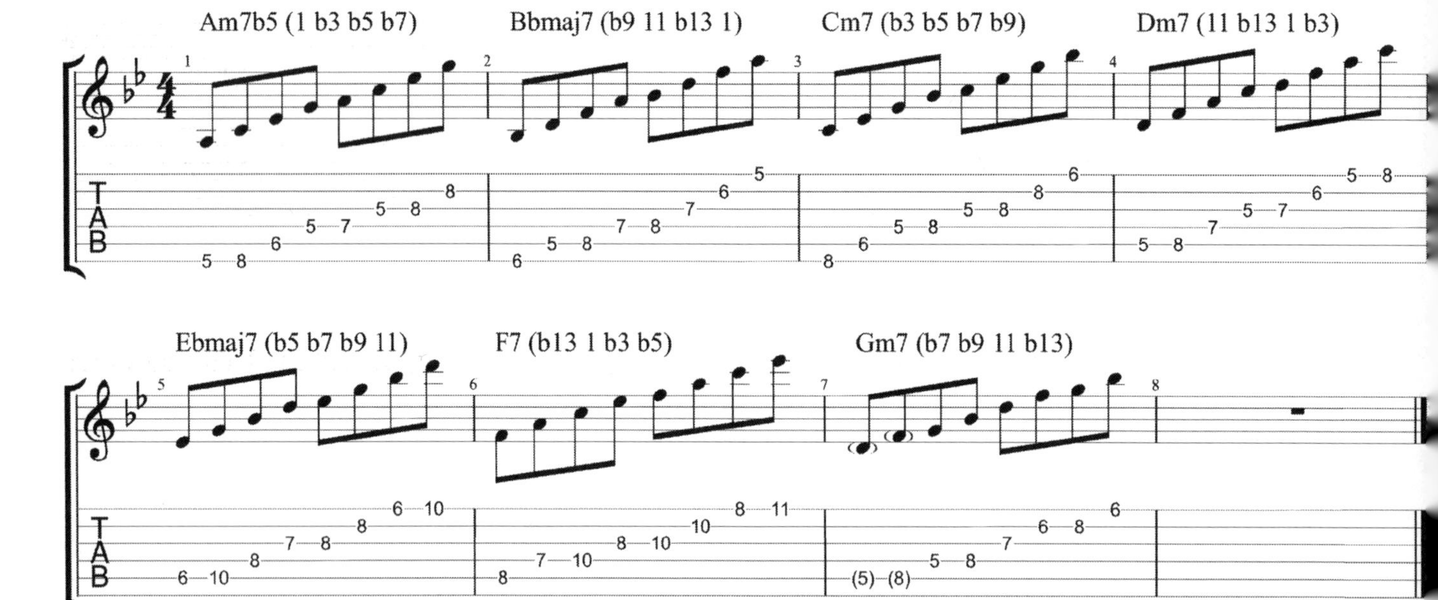

Again, you may choose to play it safe and stick with an arpeggio that is mainly chord tones of the key centre For example, playing a Minor 7 arpeggio from the b3 (C Minor 7 over A) accesses three chord tones, the b3, b5 b7, and one of the typically 'Locrian' scale degrees, the b9.

If you want to highlight the darker extensions, you may like the sound of a Minor 7 arpeggio on the b7 (G Mino 7 over A) (b7, b9, 11, b13).

5-Note Pentatonic Scales

Minor Pentatonic scales can be built on the b3, the b7 and the 11 of the Locrian mode. They are often my firs choice for soloing in Locrian as they help me to build strong melodic ideas over the unsettled harmony. Thes scales contain five notes of the mode so you will get more of the Locrian sound in your playing.

Playing a Minor Pentatonic on the b3 (C Minor Pentatonic over A) highlights the scale degrees b3, b5, b7, b9, b13. I think this is a good choice because it sticks closely to the tonic m7b5 arpeggio and adds in just two other Locrian scale tones.

Example 17r: Minor Pentatonic on b3:

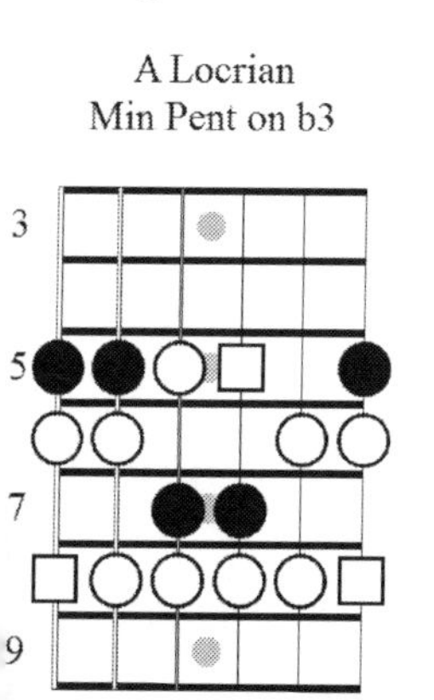

Playing a Minor Pentatonic scale from the b7 targets the scale degrees b3, b5, b7, b9 and 11. This also works well.

Example 17s: Minor Pentatonic on b7:

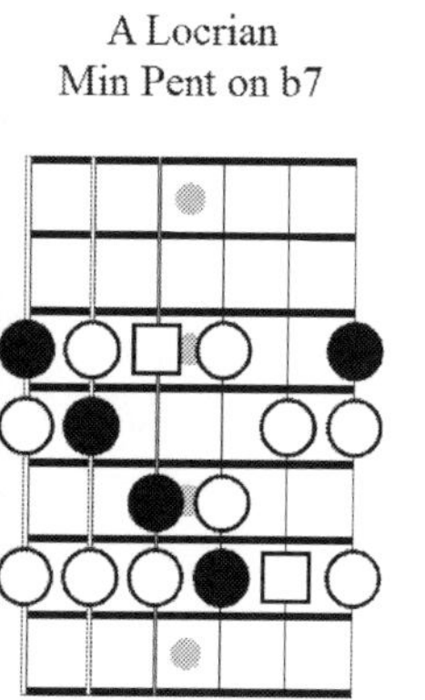

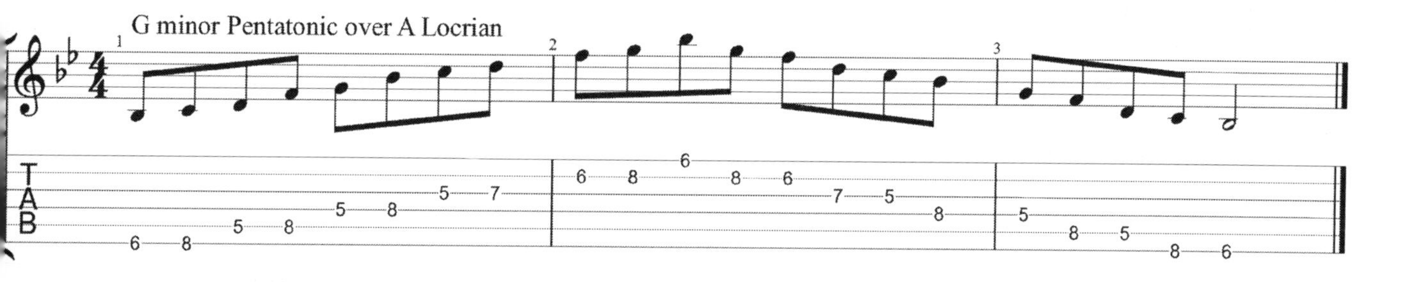

Finally, a Minor Pentatonic scale on the 11/4 targets the intervals **1, b3, b7, 11, b13.**

Example 17t: Minor Pentatonic on 11/4

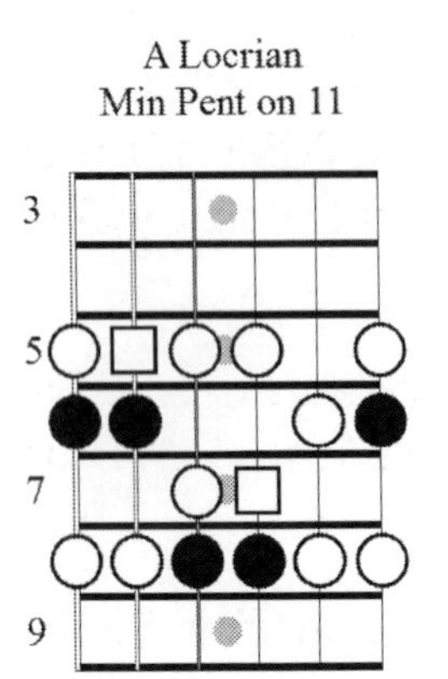

First Choice Soloing Summary for the Locrian Mode

It's hard to give first choices for the Locrian mode. The harmony is so unsettled that my best advice is to try everything and if you like it, stick with it. For the sake of completeness my first choices are:

Parent Scale: Locrian.

Intervals: 3rds and 4ths.

Triad: Major triad on the b5 / Minor triad on the the b7.

Arpeggio: Minor 7 arpeggio on the b7.

Pentatonic: Minor Pentatonic on b3 and b7.

Conclusions and Practice Tips

There is a great deal of conceptual information in this book which I have tried to make practical with specific examples and licks. However, the only way to begin to internalise this information is to play it.

Start small by picking just one mode you'd like to experiment with. I'd recommend Dorian, Mixolydian or Aeolian if you're new to these ideas. Learn the licks in the book and improvise over the backing tracks before tackling the theoretical information.

When you're comfortable making melodies with the scale over a backing track, try experimenting with my suggested first-choice interval patterns. Stick with these intervals for a few weeks and then move on to the pentatonic ideas before finally isolating individual triad and arpeggio approaches.

The important thing is to hear the different sounds that each conceptual approach will generate. You will be surprised how the textures of your solos change by focusing on each one. Even in some of the common modes like Dorian, a wide intervallic approach like playing in 6ths is ear-catching and sounds very different than superimposing Pentatonics.

Your favourite approaches will probably be different than mine. That's great and sets us apart as musicians.

One beneficial practice idea is to take a single concept and literally write ten licks with just that idea. Ask yourself how can you combine that isolated concept with other soloing approaches to create a cohesive musical line.

It is important to experiment with rhythm too. There are thousands of different ways to approach just three notes. Again, take one concept and play it with different rhythms and in different positions. You will quickly find something unique to your own voice.

The important thing is not to spread yourself too thin in your studies. It is better to play two or three ideas well, rather than twenty-three ideas poorly.

I hope the ideas in this book help to inspire your improvisations in new and exciting ways. Go slow and have fun.

Joseph.

Other Books from Fundamental Changes

The Complete Guide to Playing Blues Guitar Book One: Rhythm Guitar

The Complete Guide to Playing Blues Guitar Book Two: Melodic Phrasing

The Complete Guide to Playing Blues Guitar Book Three: Beyond Pentatonics

The Complete Guide to Playing Blues Guitar Compilation

The CAGED System and 100 Licks for Blues Guitar

Minor ii V Mastery for Jazz Guitar

Jazz Blues Soloing for Guitar

Guitar Scales in Context

Guitar Chords in Context

The First 100 Chords for Guitar

Jazz Guitar Chord Mastery

Complete Technique for Modern Guitar

Funk Guitar Mastery

The Complete Technique, Theory & Scales Compilation for Guitar

Sight Reading Mastery for Guitar

Rock Guitar Un-CAGED

The Practical Guide to Modern Music Theory for Guitarists

Beginner's Guitar Lessons: The Essential Guide

Chord Tone Soloing for Jazz Guitar

Chord Tone Soloing for Bass Guitar

Voice Leading Jazz Guitar

Guitar Fretboard Fluency

The Circle of Fifths for Guitarists

First Chord Progressions for Guitar

The First 100 Jazz Chords for Guitar

100 Country Licks for Guitar

Pop & Rock Ukulele Strumming

Walking Bass for Jazz and Blues

Guitar Finger Gym

The Melodic Minor Cookbook

The Chicago Blues Guitar Method

Heavy Metal Rhythm Guitar

Heavy Metal Lead Guitar

Progressive Metal Guitar

Heavy Metal Guitar Bible

Exotic Pentatonic Soloing for Guitar

The Complete Jazz Guitar Soloing Compilation

The Jazz Guitar Chords Compilation

Fingerstyle Blues Guitar

The Complete DADGAD Guitar Method

Country Guitar for Beginners

Beginner Lead Guitar Method

The Country Fingerstyle Guitar Method

Beyond Rhythm Guitar

Rock Rhythm Guitar Playing

Fundamental Changes in Jazz Guitar

Neo-Classical Speed Strategies for Guitar

100 Classic Rock Licks for Guitar

The Beginner's Guitar Method Compilation

100 Classic Blues Licks for Guitar

The Country Guitar Method Compilation

Country Guitar Soloing Techniques

Made in the USA
Middletown, DE
13 February 2020